Archibald Hamilton Charteris

The New Testament Scriptures

Their Claims, History, and Authority; being the Croall lectures for 1882

Archibald Hamilton Charteris

The New Testament Scriptures
Their Claims, History, and Authority; being the Croall lectures for 1882

ISBN/EAN: 9783744735674

Printed in Europe, USA, Canada, Australia, Japan

Cover: Foto ©Lupo / pixelio.de

More available books at **www.hansebooks.com**

NEW TESTAMENT SCRIPTURES:

THEIR CLAIMS, HISTORY, AND AUTHORITY.

BEING

The Croall Lectures for 1882.

BY

A. H. CHARTERIS, D.D.,

PROFESSOR OF BIBLICAL CRITICISM AND BIBLICAL ANTIQUITIES IN THE UNIVERSITY
OF EDINBURGH, AND ONE OF HER MAJESTY'S CHAPLAINS.

AUTHOR OF 'CANONICITY, BASED ON KIRCHHOFER'S QUELLENSAMMLUNG,' ETC.

.

LONDON:
JAMES NISBET & CO., 21 BERNERS STREET.
1882.

LATELY PUBLISHED,

In large 8vo, pp. 638, price 18s.,

CANONICITY:

A Collection of Early Testimonies to the Canonical Books of the New Testament, based on Kirchhofer's 'Quellensammlung.' By A. H. CHARTERIS, D.D., Professor of Biblical Criticism and Biblical Antiquities in the University of Edinburgh, and one of Her Majesty's Chaplains. William Blackwood & Sons, Edinburgh and London.

SUMMARY OF CONTENTS.

Preface—Introduction: containing chapters on Barnabas, Clement of Rome, Hermas, Ignatius, Polycarp, Papias, Basilides, Justin Martyr, Clementine Homilies, Gospel of the Hebrews, Hegesippus, Muratorian Canon, Clement of Alexandria, Origen, the Paschal Controversy, Apocryphal Literature, the Fourth Gospel—Analytical and Chronological Index of Critics and Testimonies.

PART I.—Chap. I. Oldest Testimonies to a Collection of Sacred Books—II. Testimonies to the Canon (of later date)—III. The New Testament as a Whole—IV. The Gospels—V. The Apostolical Fathers and the Synoptists—VI.-IX. Gospels of Matthew, Mark, Luke, and John—X. The Acts of the Apostles—XI. The Epistles—XII. The Epistles of Paul—XIII.-XXXIII. Testimonies to the Remaining Books of the New Testament, Romans to Jude, each in its order—XXXIV. Apocalypse.

PART II.—Testimonies of Heathen.

PART III.—Testimonies of Heretics.

PART IV.—Extra-Canonical Gospels.

OPINIONS OF THE PRESS.

Review by Professor Dr. Christlieb, D.D., in the 'Beweis des Glaubens' (February 1881).

Wenn auch zeitweise durch Krankeit etwas gehindert, hat Dr. Charteris, Professor der biblischen Kritik an der Universität Edinburg, Jahre des umsichtigsten die einschlägige deutsche und englische Literatur ausreichend benützenden Fleizes auf sein Werk verwendet, und was er uns nun bietet, verdient als *das zur Zeit präziseste und relativ zuverlässigste Nachschlagebuch für alle Zeugnisse der alten Kirche vom neutestamentl. Kanon, für alle Citate und Anklänge neutestamentl. Schriftstellen in der altchristlichen Literatur auch in Deutschland volle Beachtung.* Da aber der Preis mehr für englische als für deutsche Beutel berechnet und das umfangreiche und splendid ausgestattete Buch dem deutschen Studenten daher doppelt schwer zugänglich ist, so drängt sich uns der lebhafte Wunsch auf, dasz das Buch, etwas überarbeitet und ergänzt, ins Deutsche zurückübersetzt und in billiger Ausgabe für den Handgebrauch unserer Studierenden eingerichtet werden möchte. . . . Wir zweifeln nicht, dasz die fleissige, besonnene und sorgfältige Arbeit des verehrten Verfassers in dem gerade jetzt durch Einleitungsfragen so tief aufgeregten Schottland sehr willkommen geheiszen werden, und ob der Kampf zur Zeit auch vorwiegend um das Alte Test. tobt, doch vielen zur Beruhigung darüber dienen wird, dasz wenigstens die autorität des Neuen Test. in und auszerhalb der alten Kirche auf festem, ja gerade auch durch die neuere Kritik sich immer unerschütterlicher zeigendem Grunde ruht. Möchte darum bald dieses oder ein ähnliches Werk auch in deutscher Sprache dem Forscher zu Hülfe kommen !

From Review by Professor Godet, D.D., in the 'Revue de Theologie et de Philosophie' (Mai 1881).

Est-ce trop dire que d'affirmer l'indispensable nécessité d'un pareil écrit ? Ajoutons qu'à tous égards le livre que nous annonçons nous parait être à la hauteur de sa tâche. Les citations sont faites avec un soin, une exactitude, et une beauté typographique qui ne laisse rien à désirer. Les notes critiques qui accompagnent chaque article mettent en peu de lignes le lecteur au fait de l'état actuel de la question critique. Une connaissance approfondie des discussions les plus récentes, une appréciation toujours impartiale et judicieuse du pour et du contre distinguent ces courts exposés critiques dans lesquels nous n'avons pas surpris un mot qui ne fasse honneur à l'érudition et à la sagesse de l'auteur.

Nous croyons savoir que M. Charteris se prépare à publier un nouveau volume dans lequel il traitera des principes en vertu desquels l'Eglise a adopté les écrits dont se compose le Nouveau Testament et de l'autorité de ce recueil. Nous souhaitons à l'auteur force et lumière pour amener à bien cette nouvelle œuvre d'un caractère plus populaire ; mais nous désirerions avant tout, pour le progrès des études critiques en France, que le volume *Canonicity* fût reproduit sans trop tarder dans notre langue. Ce ne serait en majeure partie qu'une réimpression des textes cités ; quant aux résumés critiques, ils sont courts et clairs, et n'offriraient aucune difficulté de traduction.

From Review by Professor Dr. Hilgenfeld in his 'Zeitschrift fur Wissenschaftliche Theologie,' 2 Heft, 1881.

[A Review of 'Supernatural Religion ;' 'Canonicity ;' Ezra Abbot on 'The Fourth Gospel.']

In der Blüthezeit des englischen Deismus der englische Prediger Nathanael Lardner ein apologetisches Werk verfasst : 'The Credibility of the Gospel History, or the Facts occasionally mentioned by the Ancient Authors' (London 1727, u. ö.). In der Blüthezeit der Strauss'ischen Kritik des 'Lebens Jesu' hat der Schaffhausener Theolog Johannes Kirchhofer für das deutsche Sprachgebiet etwas Aehnliches versucht durch seine 'Quellensammlung zur Geschichte des Neutestamentlichen Canons bis auf Hieronymus' (Zürich 1872). Jetzt bietet der Professor der Biblischen Kritik und der Biblischen Alterthümer in Edinburgh, Herr Dr. A. H. Charteris, für das Englische Sprachgebiet eine Art von neuer Auflage der Kirchhofer'schen 'Quellensammlung.' Er hat sich freilich auch in Anderen Büchern, auch in den meinigen, umgesehen und die genannte 'Quellensammlung' wesentlich verbessert, wofür ihm auch von Unsereinem Dank gebührt. . . . So viel man auch einzureden hat, man bekommt doch eine wesentlich vollständige Sammlung der Zeugnisse welche hier in Frage Kommen. . . . So kann mann auch sonst aus diesem fleissig gearbeiteten Buche das Eine oder das Andere lernen. . . . Der Gesammteindruck, welchen die drei zusammengefassten Schriften Machen, ist in mancher Hinsicht erfreulich. Die Kritischen Fragen über den Ursprung des Christenthum's welche die Deutsche Theologen unsers Jahrhunderts so mächtig bewegt haben, setzen jetzt auch die Theologen des Englischen Sprachgebietes in lebhafte Bewegung. In den Verhandlungen erkennt man in Allgemeinen Ernst und Grundlichkeit. In einer Hinsicht müssen wir den Theologen des Englischen Sprachgebietes sogar den Vorzug zuerkennen. Die Verhandlungen werden mit wissenschaftlichen Anstande geführt, welchen wir in deutschen Sprachgebiete so oft zu vermissen hatten.

From Review by Professor C. W. Hodge, D.D., in the 'Presbyterian Review' (New York).

Professor Charteris has admirably supplied a great want, for even were Kirchhofer not out of print, the great advances in the study of these sources of proof of the Canon require new treatment. . . . The name of the work is happily chosen, being more precise than Lardner's *Credibility*, and more concise than Kirchhofer's *Quellensammlung zur Geschichte des N. T. Canons.* . . . The introduction is taken up with excellent encyclopædic articles on 'The Literature of the Authors.'

British and Foreign Evangelical Review.

What Kirchhofer did for Lardner, Dr. Charteris has done for Kirchhofer. . . . Professor Charteris writes in perfect consciousness of the most recent utterances of all kinds. He has not disdained to learn from the acute author of *Supernatural Religion*, to say nothing of Renan and Davidson. . . . The book is a fine testimony to the patience and thoroughness of the compiler ; and although very different theories will be drawn, from the data here afforded, by thinkers of various schools, for some years to come, the book must be invaluable to every student of the early testimonies to the canonical books. Like all useful books, this work upon Canonicity will enable its possessor to dispense with consulting many volumes, and will abbreviate study. . . . Altogether, this book must be indispensable to all who would have well-grounded opinions upon the authenticity of the books of the New Testament.

British Quarterly Review.

Dr. Charteris has devoted nearly 200 pages to a succinct and scholarly sketch of the documents and sources from which our ideas of a New Testament canon are derived. . . . As far as we have yet been able to test the workmanship, it is scholarly and sound, and is abreast of the latest literature on the subject.

Expositor.

Dr. Charteris has rendered no slight service to scholars by collecting in a single volume the testimony to the authorship and authenticity of the several New Testament Scriptures, and to their early admission into the Canon, which lies scattered through an innumerable array of volumes, many of which are rare or difficult of access.

Glasgow Herald.

Executed with a thoroughness and a learning not a little creditable to Scotland.

John Bull.

Indispensable to the completeness of any library which pretends to comprehensiveness and scholarship.

Notes and Queries.

The question which suggests itself first is the relation which this volume, prepared with so much thought and care, bears to a kindred work by Professor Westcott—the *General Survey of the History of the New Testament*. The writers of both are engaged on the same materials, with the same purpose ; but Dr. Charteris, whose volume is the larger one, appears to have this advantage in the form of his work,—he has been able to place the collateral information required for explanation in separate chapters at the beginning, which are followed by the testimonies themselves, arranged in order under the several books of the New Testament, in full type as the text, and not in the smaller type of the notes. By this means the authorities attain their due prominence, and their evidence is easily ascertained.

The Churchman.

A work of singular value, based on Kirchhofer. . . . The learned Professor has made good use of all the helps possible ; but his judgment and accuracy are as remarkable as his research.

The Christian Church.

The materials are, of course, for the most part common : but Dr. Charteris has not been content simply to reproduce them. On the contrary, as we have ascertained by a careful collation of the work with that of Kirchhofer, in numerous passages taken at random, the citations have been revised, corrected, enlarged, supplemented, and rearranged with a minute care which can only be appreciated by those who take the trouble so to compare them. . . . Nothing can well exceed the fairness and candour with which Dr. Charteris states the arguments, marshals the facts, and gives his own impression of their significance. . . . We may not omit a word of acknowledgment for the admirable form of the book as regards the beauty and clearness of its printing, for the numerous devices of displayed and italicized type, headings, references, and cross references, by which its use is facilitated, and for the copious and careful indexes, for which Dr. Charteris owns himself indebted to the friendly aid of former students.

Westminster Review.

Notwithstanding our frequent and profound dissent from some of the views advocated in Professor Charteris' collection of early testimonies of the New Testament writings, entitled *Canonicity*, we thankfully accept his work.

Lutheran Quarterly (New York).

Well suited to fill the place which it has been meant to supply, being marked as it is throughout by scholarly ability, careful research, and critical discrimination.

PREFACE.

THE following Lectures are printed as they were delivered. They are an attempt to answer questions which are often put as to the claims of the Christian Scriptures on the Christian believer's acceptance. I have endeavoured to divest the subject of technicality, and to write for those who are unable or who have not leisure to study the copious literature of the subject. The references to books are almost all to such as are easily accessible. In treating of the early witnesses to the claims and the authority of the books of the New Testament, I have necessarily made statements without being able to adduce the evidence in detail. Instead of defending or illustrating such general statements in Notes at the end of the volume, as is usually done in published lectures, I have ventured in footnotes to refer to the evidence which I have already compiled for students in a recently published work, entitled *Canonicity*. In so far as concerns the history of the New Testament Canon, these Lectures may serve as a popular guide to the results of an examination of the testimonies arranged in that book. Many friends and critics have suggested the preparation of such a guide, and I shall be glad if this meet their wishes.

DATES OF SOME OF THE PRINCIPAL WRITERS AND WRITINGS NOTICED.

CONTENTS.

LECTURE I.

LECTURE II.

LECTURE V.

LECTURE VI.

LECTURE I.

THE first step to be taken in an investigation into the rightful place of New Testament Scripture, is to inquire what it *claims* to be. It is unreasonable to begin by considering what it ought to be, or must be. Nor is it advantageous even to consider in the first place what it is—this New Testament with which we are so familiar. Those books — what are they ? a most proper question ; but, first of all, Those books—what do they claim to be ?

In asking this question, we assume generally the existence of a Canon of Holy Scripture ; for it is a fact that such a Canon has been handed down to us from bygone days. The evidence on which any particular book was received into the Canon does not meanwhile concern us. An examination of that evidence may be needed in order to test the claims of such a book to be part of Scripture, but our first concern is with the Canon as a whole.

1. And first, we observe that all the books of the New Testament, like those of Scripture

A

generally, claim to be *true*. The writers of
Scripture profess that they write no cunningly
devised fables. From the beginning of St.
Matthew's Gospel to the end of Jude,—we may
even say to the end of the Apocalypse,—all
professes to be true. Taking no higher ground
than that of the ground of historical accuracy, we
have to remember that no writer asks for himself
less consideration than St. Luke, who wrote his
Gospel that 'Theophilus might know the *certainty*
of those things in which he had been instructed.'
When an attempt is made to treat the incidents
of the Gospels as myths or legends, a violent hand
is laid upon the narratives, because the writers
themselves evidently proceed on the statements as
facts.   When the endeavour is to separate the
doctrine from the history, as we distinguish in
Æsop between the moral and the fable, it is a
bootless effort, because the gospel doctrine is the
doctrine of a Life, so that the doctrine stands or
falls with the facts.   The faith of Christendom is
fixed on the living Lord of the Church, and that
faith cannot be now retained, any more than it
could be retained in St. Paul's day, unless the
history of Christ's resurrection be true.   'If Christ
be not risen, then our faith is vain.'   The doctrines of the Scripture are inseparably blended
with the historical narratives ; and these histories,
if they be false, drag down with them into their

pit of error the doctrines also, however holy and dear those may be. But alike for the narratives and the doctrinal statements which they contain, the books of the New Testament claim that they are true.

2. Further, those books claim for themselves *Unity*. The books of Scripture are a series, not a congeries. This is true of the Bible as a whole, and is the most remarkable fact in literature as well as in religion. I am not aware that the sacred books of any other creed contain anything that can even be compared with it. In the long history of one family, a consistent revelation is expanded, developed, and completed, being the teaching of a Father who gave the truth to His children as they were able to take it in. In this the two Testaments are alike—each in relation to the parts which compose it. In the Old Testament the history of the chosen people follows step by step from the call of Abraham, through the legislation of the Pentateuch and the annals of the kingdom, with psalms and prophets filling up with light and song the rapid sketch given in the narrative of the nation's laws and sins. In the New Testament, in like manner, each part is linked with each from the birth of Jesus Christ, through His mighty life and His mightier death and rising again, and through the marvels that His Church did and saw when His Spirit came, on to the vision

of the future day in which the seer saw His second coming to reign. We need not pause to prove that the Epistles are a continuation of the Gospels, or to show how inseparable are the facts of the Acts of the Apostles from the assertions of the Pauline Epistles. The connection is too obvious to be overlooked. Thus is each Testament as a whole composed of parts which spring out of each other. In the same way the two Testaments are connected with each other. St. Matthew's Gospel connects the appearance of Christ with the faith of ancient Israel, and the Epistles develop the doctrines of Christianity in living connection with the types and the foreshadowings of the former dispensation. The ancient prophet said : ' Thou, Israel, art my servant, Jacob whom I have chosen, the seed of Abraham my friend. Thou whom I have taken from the ends of the earth, and called thee from the chief men thereof, and said unto thee, Thou art my servant ; I have chosen thee, and not cast thee away ' (Isa. xli. 8). In like manner the apostle said of Israel, ' that blindness in part is happened to them till the fulness of the Gentiles be come in. . . . As concerning the gospel, they are enemies for your sakes : but as touching the election, they are beloved for the fathers' sakes. For the gifts and calling of God are without repentance ' (Rom. xi. 29).

Let us dwell for a moment on what this unity

implies. I have spoken of it as a historical unity, a unity of fact and purpose, linked like one long chain through all the ages during which the book was being made in the lives of redeemed and sanctified men. But this is not all. There is an absolute perpetuity of doctrine throughout Scripture. The Jews were a people as prone to sensual indulgence, to infidelity, and to idolatry as any other people, and yet in the midst of them grew up the revelation of holy law and spiritual worship and self-denying purity of life, out of which, in the 'fulness of the times,' there grew, as a fruitful branch from a living root, the marvellous manifestation of God in the gospel of His Son. Our purpose is to deal with the books of the New Testament, but we cannot forget that they not only *claim* to stand in the same unity with each other, but to be parts of a unity which contains in it the whole old covenant as well. It is not the unity of a consistent speculation, or of a logical statement, which might have been the work of some peculiarly qualified men at a particular date. It is not the unity of a school of philosophy where the master's spirit almost unconsciously moves his disciples. It is a unity of action and experience, as well as of thought and purpose and aspiration; a unity revealed in a marvellous history as well as in a marvellous book. It is a unity like that of the light of heaven, which is one because its source is one. It is, in short, the unity of the revealing God, who at sundry times and in divers manners spake in time past unto the fathers by the prophets, but in the last days spake unto men by His Son. This is the claim in Matt. v. 17, and of Heb. i.

The doctrine, that there is one living God, is that to which thought has brought thinkers; but the strange pre-eminence of the Bible lies in this being from the first unto the last the doctrine of which its whole teaching is full. In the ancient days, when Assyria was finding a separate spirit in every power of nature and in almost every natural object, and when Phœnicia was adoring the sun as the primary power of all things, Abraham and his seed offered the homage of their love to the Eternal Spirit who of old made the world and all things that creep and fly in it, and who set the sun to rule the day and the moon to rule the night. The idea which had currency not long ago, that the Semitic nations were Monotheists in virtue of a superior mental constitution, has been scattered like a morning dream by recent researches. The whole of the Semitic tribes—as, for example, the Moabites, Ammonites, and Babylonians—seem to have been incapable of rising to the great doctrine of the unity and spirituality of God, the living God. But that doctrine is the key-note of the Scripture from first to last. The

Monotheism of the Israelites stands alone in history.[1] It is neither the Monotheism of Egypt, which, like the worship of Phœnicia, was a kind of solar Pantheism; nor like that of Persia, later in date, which was really Dualism; nor like that of ancient India, where worship was broken up into invocations of many gods, each successively addressed as supreme. There is nothing in ancient or in modern religions outside of the Bible which can for a moment compare with the revelation made in Horeb to Moses, a revelation that was so often the burden of prophetic cry in the after days: 'The Lord, the Lord God, merciful and gracious, long-suffering and abundant in goodness and truth.' This unity has no parallel—the unity of the succession of books which all tell in letter and in spirit of one God, the living and the loving God.

Nor will it avail to reply to this, that the unity is not so marvellous as it seems, because the books are the forgeries or inventions of one particular epoch. We must not attempt to reason on the subject of the Old Testament, because it would turn us from the primary object of those lectures; but it is a simple matter of fact that every critic, even of the most destructive school, who attempts anything constructive in regard to the composition of the Old Testament, has to lay down as the basis

[1] On the religion of the ancient Eastern nations, see Auberlen's *Divine Revelation*, p. 126, and Max Müller, *Hist. of Sansk. Lit.*, chap. iv., especially p. 558.

of his system that, whatever be the date at which
the books were written, the nation and the national
life of Israel sprang from faith in the covenant
God, who had chosen the fathers, and was fulfilling
His promise unto their children.[1] But let us turn
to the New Testament. We can see in the books
which compose it organic unity of such a kind as
to warrant us in inferring from one portion the
general nature of the whole, as an anatomist can
tell from one bone what the skeleton has been.
The second quarter of this century saw the rise
and culmination of a singularly learned, able, and
adventurous school of New Testament critics,—the
Tübingen School, — whose main tenet was that
Christianity grew into its present shape under the
influence of various conflicting tendencies among
which it was a compromise. They set aside its
supernatural character; they regard its predictions
as written after the events, and the miracles as
exaggerations of facts which did actually occur, or
as legends invented by a conviction that such
things must have been because they were necessary to complete men's ideas of The Christ. They
maintain that the books were not written till long
after the events, till dreams and legends had time
to grow into their present shape. That is what
men are now maintaining as to the Old Testament;
but we are speaking of the school which some

[1] This may be seen in the systems of Reuss, Wellhausen, etc.

forty years ago applied those ideas to the New
Testament, and especially to the Life of Christ in
the Gospels. But the ablest and clearest of them
all—Baur himself—allowed that four of St. Paul's
letters and the Apocalypse of John were genuine.
And we need no more than this to show that the
whole system is untenable. For what do we find ?
We find in those Epistles, themselves of the very
earliest date, all the leading characteristics of the
Christian system, which, according to the theory,
are supposed to have been the growth of the
subsequent hundred years. It is of no avail to
say that miracles and predictions had grown
around the traditional idea of Jesus Christ until
they took shape in the Gospels of our Canon during
the second century. In contradiction of that
allegation is the fact that those admittedly genuine
letters of St. Paul found upon the miracles of
Christ's life, and rest upon the Resurrection as
the primary and indispensable basis of the whole
system, as proving the triumphant close of the
incarnate life and atoning death of the Saviour.
'Paul, an apostle, not from man, neither through
man, but through Jesus Christ, and God the Father,
who raised Him from the dead' (Gal. i. 1). In those
memorable words of an admittedly genuine Epistle,
Paul claims to have been addressed, and despatched
on his mission of love and toil, by the Personal
Saviour speaking to him from on high. So, too,

he tells the Romans that the subject of the gospel
is God's Son, Jesus Christ 'our Lord, which was
made of the seed of David according to the flesh,'
—there we have the incarnation asserted as a
cardinal fact,—'and declared to be the Son of God
with power, according to the spirit of holiness, by
the resurrection from the dead' (Rom. i. 3, 4);
there we have the resurrection with power connected with the holy sinlessness of Jesus Christ.
It is perfectly clear that the gospel which Paul
believed and preached was the same gospel that
is preserved for us by our canonical Evangelists.

Nor is this all. See how St. Paul charges and
challenges his very opponents to consider not only
the miracles of the life of Christ, but the miracles
which attested the truth of apostolic preaching.
'O foolish Galatians, who did bewitch you, before
whose eyes Jesus Christ was openly set forth
crucified? . . . He therefore that supplieth to you
the Spirit, and *worketh miracles* among you, doeth
he it by the works of the law, or by the hearing
of faith?' (Gal. iii. 1, 5). Here is an appeal to
miracles as to manifest facts with which the
Galatians were familiar, which they had experi-
enced ; yea, which some of their own number were
working.[1] In the same way he says to the Corin-

---

[1] The Greek participles 'supplying' and 'ministering' may be imperfect, and may mean ' He therefore that supplied to you the Spirit, and
worked miracles among you '—at that time when ye received the Spirit
(ver. 2). But it is perhaps more natural to regard the words as in

thians divided against themselves, and disparaging
him : 'Truly the signs of an apostle were wrought
among you in all patience, by signs, and wonders,
and mighty works' (2 Cor. xii. 12).   We need to
bear in mind that those passages were no rhetorical
outbursts, but were in each case the very point of
an earnest argument addressed to unfriendly men.
The Galatians had fallen away from the faith which
Paul preached among them; were in fact opposed
to him ; some of them were even turning him to
ridicule ; and the apostle seeks to bring them back
to a true position by appealing to the well-known
facts of miraculous power (δυνάμεις) with which
they were familiar.   'Can you apostatize (he
says) from a faith based on indisputable miracles
wrought among you?'   Had such miracles not
been wrought, would Paul have dared to appeal
to them as evidence ?   Nor was this an argument
addressed only to the impressible Celts of Galatia.
We have seen that when he wrote to the culti-
vated and practised disputants of Achaia, who
did not own his apostolical authority, he said in
words of the same purport : 'Ye Corinthians know
very well that I wrought miracles, and signs, and
wonders among you, and am I, then, not an
apostle ?'

Now, a man may reject the book of the Acts of
present time, and if so, the inference is irresistible that some of the
Galatians were using miraculous endowments at the time when the
apostle wrote.

the Apostles ever so summarily ; but if he admits the genuineness of the Epistles to Galatia, Rome, and Corinth, he must admit that the men to whom Paul wrote—even those of them who were his enemies—were fully convinced of the miraculous gifts of the apostles, and had seen them in the midst of their daily life.

If time permitted, it could be proved of Christian doctrine that the germ of every doctrine is found in any one of those Epistles, and indeed in every one of the principal books of the New Testament ; so that in a hundred positive statements and a thousand undesigned coincidences the marvellous unity of the Christian Scriptures is clearly seen. And it is so seen as to show, that not only are the events recorded in the Gospels necessary precursors of the allusions and appeals of the Epistles, but the evangelic narratives themselves are proved by their simplicity of structure and statement, and by their mode of recording facts without drawing doctrinal conclusions, to be substantially earlier than the more systematized and developed teaching of the apostolic letters.   It is inconceivable that anything so simple, direct, and so devoid of any statement of inferences as any one of our Synoptic Gospels could be the sequel of the Pauline Epistles, and be written to account for them or to sustain them.   All the rules of literary probability are violated when the narratives of the gospel—or, let us say, narratives so nearly identical with our Synoptic Gospels that no discrepancy whatever can be established—are not admitted as the 'gospel' which Paul preached (1 Cor. xv. 1).

Not only, therefore, do we find unity of statement and of doctrine, but a unity with a historical development in the books of the New Testament. To what other collection of writings, composed by so many men during so many years, and in circumstances so diverse, can such unity be ascribed?

3. Again, the writers of those books claim *Authority*. They do not seem to contemplate the possibility of being in error, whether they speak of things past, present, or to come; and they do not admit that any man can be justified who disobeys their teachings. 'Though we or an angel from heaven should preach unto you any gospel other than that which we preached unto you, let him be anathema' (Gal. i. 8). Peter admonishes his Jewish brethren to be mindful not more of 'the words which were spoken before by the holy prophets' than of 'the commandments of the Lord and Saviour through your apostles' (2 Peter iii. 2). And perhaps the most suggestive words of all are those of St. Paul: 'Which things also we speak, not in words which man's wisdom teacheth, but which the Holy Spirit teacheth; comparing spiritual things with spiritual' (1 Cor. ii. 13). Again, he thanks God that when the Thessalonians received

from him the message, even the words of God,
they accepted it, 'not as the words of men, but, as
it is in truth, the word of God' (1 Thess. ii. 13).
If, as is commonly believed, the Thessalonian
Epistles are the oldest of St. Paul's writings, we
have a special significance in the words of 1 Thess.
v. 27, which solemnly enjoin the public reading of
his letters in public Christian worship: 'I adjure
you by the Lord that this Epistle be read unto all
the brethren' (1 Thess. v. 27).   So also 2 Thess.
ii. 15, iii. 12; Eph. ii. 20.

There is a passage which has been sometimes
founded upon as though it drew a distinction
between words which came on St. Paul's own
authority and those which had the direct authority
of God.   But in the chapter referred to (1 Cor. vii.)
the apostle is not distinguishing between God's
commandments and his own teachings, but between
the things which he was authorized to teach for the
first time and those in which he was repeating the
decisions of the Lord Jesus Christ in the days of
His flesh.[1]   In the last verse he winds up the

---

[1] The passages in 1 Cor. vii. to which reference is here made are:
Ver. 10—'Unto the married I give charge, *yet not I, but the Lord*, That
the wife depart not from her husband; . . . and let not the husband
put away his wife.' The Lord gave His clear commandment against
separation of spouses on any ground save that of adultery in Matt. v. 32
and xix. 6-9. Ver. 12—'But to the rest *say I, not the Lord*: If any
brother hath an unbelieving wife,' etc. That is, the case of a Christian
whose spouse did not become a Christian is new since the days of the
Lord in the flesh, and the apostle of the Lord is under the necessity of
providing for it. Ver. 25—'Now concerning virgins I *have no com-*

subject with the statement that a widow will be happier if she do not marry again. This, he says, is his own judgment as to expediency, formed on his observation of life,—it is no matter of invariable right and wrong,—and he has good reason to know (his claim is an approved claim) that he also has the Spirit of God.

We have been dealing only with the New Testament, but in the Old Testament also we find strong claims to authority : 'The word of the Lord came unto Zechariah, saying, Thus speaketh the Lord of hosts.' 'Truly,' says Micah, 'I am full of power by the Spirit of the Lord, and of judgment, and of might, to declare unto Jacob his transgression, and to Israel his sins' (Micah iii. 8).[1]

The prophets prophesied amid prevailing incre-

---

mandment of the Lord, but *I give my judgment*, as one that hath obtained mercy of the Lord to be faithful.' St. Paul cannot quote here a direct commandment of the Lord. The circumstances of the Church were special. Neither through His voice in the days of His flesh, nor by His Spirit when the apostle wrote, had Christ given any general commandment ; but Paul, as an apostle whom grace made a 'faithful' steward of the divine mysteries (see Acts ix. 15, xxii. 15, xxvi. 10 ; 1 Cor. iv. 1, 2), was empowered to give a suggestion or recommendation. It was not a thing for commandments ; it was a thing for 'permission' (ver. 6). The powers and natures of men varied so much that no general rule could be laid down. This is explicitly said in verses 6 and 36, 37. Ver. 40—'I give my judgment (as in ver. 25), and I claim (here as in the matter of ver. 25) the well-approved position of one who also has the Spirit of God.' Our Revised Version translates by 'I think' two totally different words—νομίζω (ver. 25) and δοκῶ (ver. 40), but δοκῶ has in the New Testament the force which is given in 'claim an approved (or admitted) position.' The Revisers partially admit this by translating it 'reputed' in Gal. ii. 9.

[1] See the first words of Jeremiah, Ezekiel, Joel, Malachi ; also, Jer. xi. 13 ; Micah iv. 4 ; Hosea xii. 10, 11 ; Amos iii. 7 ; and Jer. xxix. 8.

dulity (Ezek. xii. 21), and oftentimes had to take precautions to secure the record of their words (Isa. viii. 1–16), and even to face personal dangers (Jer. xxvi. 11). They claim, nevertheless, to have supernatural manifestations of the divine will made unto them ; to be under constraint to declare the truth which has been thus revealed to them. And when we remember the pure morality which those messages convey, the unbounded trust in the living God which they inculcate and exemplify, it is impossible to believe that the prophets were either deceivers or self-deceived.

We have also to remember that, while most of the prophecies claim to have been spoken by the direct and specific command of God, some of them claim for themselves that they were not only spoken but written by divine authority. Whether they were originally spoken or written, it is clear that, as eventually written, they make for themselves this assertion of an authority more than human. Nor is this true only of prophecies, since in many cases the same claim is advanced in the historical books. Thus in the Old Testament Jehovah said : 'Write this for a memorial' (Ex. xvii. 14 ; Num. xxxiii. 1). The written law is appointed as a subject of study for the captain of Israel (Joshua i. 7, 8). Compare Ex. xxiv. 4 and Deut. xxxi. 24. In a later book the earlier books are called 'Scripture of Truth,' which mortals study and angels are sent to expound (Dan. x. 21, ix. 2). To this claim of the Old Testament the Saviour set His seal when He said : 'Moses wrote of me' (John v. 46). And he who most resembled the prophets of the Old Testament, the seer of the Apocalypse, is commanded on twelve different occasions to write in a book, and those writings are called the true sayings of God. The Lord the God of the spirit of the prophets sent His angel to show His servants in Christian times the things which must shortly come to pass (Rev. xxii. 6).

Thus there is a claim of authority advanced, not only on behalf of the men, but on behalf of the books. But have not similar claims been advanced in behalf of other books counted divine by great sections of the human family? We believe that such a claim is not made in those other works themselves. The Bible, addressing itself to all men as a revelation, claims truth, unity, and authority. Is this so with other sacred books? The great German scholar who on English ground has done so much to advance both in popular interest and in scientific grasp the twin subjects of comparative philology and comparative religion, speaking against the attempt to classify historical religions as natural and revealed, says that the classification is useless for scientific purposes, and adds : 'A more extended study shows us very soon that the claim of revelation is set up by the founders, or if not by them, at

B

all events by the later preachers and advocates of
most religions, and would therefore be declined by
all but ourselves as a distinguishing feature of
Christianity and Judaism.'[1]

When we look closely at those words they are
seen to admit of an inquiry which they do not
suggest.   It appears that in some cases the ' claim
of revelation' may not have been made by the
founders, but only by the later preachers and
advocates of the particular religion. If, however,
it was not made by the founder and first preachers,
it is not parallel to the claim of the New Testament.   We have seen that Christ Himself and
the apostles claimed that their words were authoritative.   We might have showed that the same is
true of the organs of revelation in the Old Testament.   Do we find the same to be true of other
religions ?   The sacred books of many of the great
religions of the world are now happily within the
reach of all of us,—thanks to Professor Max Müller
himself and to his fellow-labourers,[2]—and we may
search them to ascertain whether the claim to be
a divine revelation is advanced in the words of the
founders, advanced to the people for whom the
religion was revealed.

But when we study the great historical religions of
the world, we find that in many of them we cannot

---

[1] Max Müller, *Lectures on the Science of Religion* (1873), p. 129.
[2] In the *Sacred Books of the East*, now in course of publication.

institute the desired comparison from the want of sacred books. Beginning with those we know best, we do not find that there ever was a book containing the religion of Greece; and scholars toilsomely hunt for allusions[1] in the battle-songs of Homer or in the speculations of Hesiod, well aware that no sacred book guided the Hellenic worshipper in the rites of his great Pantheon. Similarly there was no book to guide the devotees in Rome; legend, custom, cravings having caused the deification, and maintaining the worship, of the 30,000 divine potentates who were supposed to rule the rulers of the world. We go to ancient Egypt, where, if anywhere in the old times, religion was a power. We find sacred texts wrapping the bodies of men in high life and of men in low life. The royal pyramid seems not to have been more assuredly (although more demonstratively) the shrine of a faith in some sort of resurrection and immortality than the poor man's grave. We find in some hymns to the Sun-god words of lofty import and capable of expressing high-spirited devotion. But we not only do not find any sacred books in which God was revealed, and by which men were guided; we find that if there were a spiritual meaning in the rites of the dominant faith, it was one of which the ordinary worshipper had no con-

---

[1] See Mr. Gladstone's *Juventus Mundi* for an example of this in much detail, not leading to much conviction.

ception or dream.[1]   It was in those hymns, if
anywhere, that the standard of Egyptian religion
was contained; and even if the hymns had been
used and understood by all the worshippers, they
still could not be compared with the Bible, because
they do not claim the character and the authority
of a revelation by God to man.[2]

The sacred books of Babylonia and Assyria,[3] if
there ever were any, have not been recovered.
The earliest Accadian and the more recent Semitic
records have come only in fragments into our hands;

[1] See Rawlinson's *History of Ancient Egypt*, vol. i., for a high estimate
of the esoteric religion of Egypt. See Wilkinson's *Ancient Egyptians*
(Birch), vol. ii. p. 471 ff., for proofs of its want of power over the people.

[2] It is beside our present point to dwell upon the fact that even in the
Ritual of the Dead (which is, in part at least, the oldest Egyptian religious document), with its picture of the scene when the soul leaves the
body, we have no divine view of sin, but an extremely human, imperfect, and superficial view; so that the soul is actually imagined as able
to maintain innocence of each sin laid to his charge before the Judge,
and as entitled, in virtue of this innocence, to entrance on the more
immediate presence of the Great Osiris. The 'forty-and-two' avengers
or accusers, each one a personification of the sin he is waiting to avenge,
are each in succession obliged to admit that they find no fault in him.
The first of the soul's statements upon trial is: 'I have neither done
any sin nor omitted any duty to any man!' (See Lepsius' *Book of the
Dead*, with introductory translation in Bunsen's *Egypt's Place in Universal History*, vol. v.; Naville's *La Litanie du Soleil*, p. 122; Poole,
Contemp. Rev., vol. xxxix. p. 808; Wilkinson's *Ancient Egyptians*
(Birch's edition), vol. ii. pp. 471, 478.) Hardwicke's *Christ and other
Masters* (p. 26 of *Egyptian Religion*) maintains on insufficient grounds
that the ancient melodies of Egypt may be regarded as on the same
level with the Hindu Vedas and the sacred books of the Chinese. But
even if they were on that level, they could not (as we shall see) compare
with the Bible. The Litany of Ra first appears in the 19th dynasty,
about 1400 B.C.

[3] Their worship of the heavenly bodies, probably because connected
with astrology, regarded the moon as supreme; while in Egypt and
Phœnicia the sun had the chief place.

and comparison of them with the Bible, as regards their claim to be a revelation, is not possible. But we may say that, while they contain a distorted tradition of the Bible history of the Creation, the Fall, and the Deluge, and a more distinct reference to man's sins than we find in other old extra-biblical religions, they cannot be cited as claiming the character of a revelation.

Nor can any other account be given of ancient Phœnicia. On the heights of Syria, beneath the blazing sun, men like Balaam reared their altars to the great god of the sun. They adored him—Baal or Bel—as the author of light and life; but it was their view of Baal, not Baal's words to them, on which their creed and their ritual rested. There is nothing to compare with the religion of the Hebrew and of the Christian, resting on a divine revelation, given at sundry times and in divers manners by the one living God.

If in more modern times we pursue an inquiry among the heathen tribes of America, North and South, or among those of the scattered islands of the Southern Seas, we find that none of them can be said to possess a book-religion, and none of them can be compared with the religion of the Bible. They all have vague yearnings for a Great Spirit — many of them worship the spirit of departed relatives; in Mexico and in Polynesia we find traditions resembling the Bible history, — the Deluge being even there, as indeed everywhere, a great fact in the earliest memories of man,—but we do not find any book claiming to be a revelation from the Most High God.[1]

And thus we find that in some of the most powerful religions of the ancient world, and in many of the prevalent idolatries of more recent times, there is nothing to correspond with the religion of the Bible, which claims to be founded on revelation.

But this being so, let us turn to the religions which are called 'book-religions.'

Let us first take those regarding the nature of which there can be little doubt. There are three religions in China: Confucianism, Taoism, and Buddhism. Of Buddhism we shall speak afterwards ; but in regard to the other two, what do we find ? We find books of philosophy—avowed philosophy—and of social ethics ; but we do not find a claim to revelation in the original documents. It is true that here, as in Babylon, there are historical records going back to some twenty-four centuries before the Christian era, but they are not in any sense a Bible or guiding revelation ; and that here, as in Egypt, there are hymns or poems of remote antiquity, which were in the

---

[1] Mr. Milne, missionary in the New Hebrides, tells me that the Fall and the Forbidden Fruit are known among the islanders, who are of a most primitive class.

minds and mouths of men, and that Confucius
(whose date is about 500 or 600 years before
Christ) said that 'the man who did not know
the poems was like one who stands with his
face to a wall, limited in his view, and unable to advance.' But those poems are occupied
with ceremonies in the worship of ancestors, and
do not speak, save incidentally, about the worship
of God, and indeed seem to have been collected
and rewarded by kings as the prize poems of the
various provinces.[1] 'Every fifth year the Son of
Heaven made a progress through the kingdom,
when the grand music-master was commanded to
lay before him the poems of the different states as
an exhibition of the manners and government of the
people.'[2] These are not even a professed revelation. Emperors of China have counted it their
duty to write commentaries on some of the ancient
books of Confucius, — especially on one which
inculcates filial piety,—and in this and in many
other ways Confucianism is proved to be a book-
religion ; but the books themselves are avowedly
human books. 'They do not profess to be or to
contain a revelation. They speak of God's work
and guidance as any religious man might do.'[3]

Taoism is in the same position. It has books,
and noble books they are in many respects. They

---

[1] Legge, *Sacred Books of the East*, vol. iii. pp. 284, 302.
[2] *Record of Rites*, p. 291 (compiled B.C. 179–155).
[3] Legge, Introduction, p. xx.

teach the religion of a simple and pure life, whose purity begins at the heart, and is thence diffused over all the character. But although long subsequent centuries ascribed supernatural greatness to Laotse, the founder of Taoism, and though in our own time the chief of the sect is supposed to exalt and to depose at his pleasure both gods and men, his own books, like those of Confucius, though more spiritual than his, are the code and the conclusions of an earnest ethical speculator, who not only did not rest his system upon God's revelation, but who all but ignored God in every sense. His system borrows both from Confucianism and Buddhism, and is a high morality, with grotesque beliefs, which have led to mean and debasing observances.[1]

I come now to the grandest and most venerable of all to which we have access, to the gigantic system of Brahmanism, which does claim to be a revelation, with words coming from the breath of Brahma.[2] Indian sages tell us that by the divine

---

[1] See Legge's Introduction, Part III.

[2] Indian philosophers and commentators have studied the subject of revelation and inspiration in all its bearings as connected with their sacred faith, and the subtlest questions of the possible relations of evidence, whether internal or external evidence, to a divine revelation are handled with exhaustive ability and subtlety. There are curious disquisitions upon the difficulty of regarding the Vedic hymns as eternal when the words of which they consist are necessarily temporal; and recent commentators say that the Rishis (*i.e.* the poets) only *saw* the hymns in the Vedas which had existed from eternity. The most systematic, interesting, and suggestive treatment of the whole subject

word contained in the Vedas the world was made, the word, or words, being eternal, older than the creation.[1]   The Brahman alone may teach the sacred books, which, however, all men—save Sudras—must commit to memory.[2]   For Sudras and women an inferior revelation has been provided; but all the others of the race are engaged from early boyhood, with infinite pains and care, embedding in their memories the holy words, which for many centuries were unwritten, and are still found as accurately in the mouths of village priests as in manuscript or in printed book.   One thinks of Deuteronomy with its injunction : ‘These words, which I command thee this day, shall be in thine heart : and thou shalt teach them diligently unto thy children, and shalt talk of them when thou sittest in thine house, and when thou walkest by the way, and when thou liest down, and when thou risest up.   And thou shalt bind them for a sign upon thy hand, and they shall be as frontlets between thine eyes.   And thou shalt write them upon the posts of thy house, and on thy gates’ (Deut. vi. 6).   Here, at last, we are ready to say we find a religion resting upon a book as that of

of the Vedas from this point of view is in Dr. John Muir's *Sanskrit Texts*, vol. iii.   See also Ballantyne's *Christianity contrasted with Hindu Philosophy* for a view of recent speculations, p. 192 ff.

[1] See Dr. John Muir's *Sanskrit Texts*, vol. iii. p. 71.

[2] See also Colebrooke's *Misc. Essays*, vol. i. p. 305 ff.   See also Müller's *History of Ancient Sanskrit Literature*, pp. 119, 364, 388.

Israel rested, and using the book as Moses enjoined the law to be used.[1]

But it is not so upon closer inspection. Those customs and injunctions, this deifying of the sacred books, are the growth of later years. We pass up through the Upanishads or philosophy of Brahmanism, through the Brahmanas or ceremonial and ritual of Brahmanism, to the Vedic hymns on which the whole fabric rests, and we find that while the later books—commentaries, meditations, and regulations — do claim in the most emphatic terms divine sanction for the Vedic hymns, those hymns claim a very different position for themselves. We find the Rishis (or authors of those hymns) appealing to the deities, and claiming favour because they have succeeded in making a good hymn, as men make a car, *Rig-Veda*, iv. 16, 20. 'O Indra [do this for him], who has generated for thee a new and exhilarating hymn, springing from an intelligent mind, an ancient mental product, full of sacred truth' (*Rig-Veda*, viii. 84). Some of the writers do claim a divine influence when making their hymns, which they themselves, curiously enough, praise as excellent, sometimes saying that the juice of the Soma exhilarated them ; and several of them claim

---

[1] The Koran similarly enjoins on men to rise in the early night and learn to recite the Koran with well-measured recitation. See *Sura* lxxiii.

inspiration from their predecessors; but in all those cases the inspiration and invocation are like that which Homer courted from the Muse in words Milton did not disdain to echo. In a hesitating way, at some complacent moment, the poets said that some god — never the Supreme Brahma, the uncreated and eternal god, but some inferior god—had enabled him to sing;[1] not even once, however, did he claim to have been the utterer of a revelation. In truth, the ancient idea of inspiration was as different from that of revelation as in our own day. The Vedas are often trifling, sometimes lofty, but there is something grotesque in the attempt to regard them as a revelation; and it is an attempt which cannot survive a perusal of the original hymns themselves.

The religion of the Medes and Persians, who overthrew Babylon, is known as Zoroastrianism or Parsism, and although its adherents, even in India, are now few and diminished, while in Persia it is not held save by the population of a few villages, it claims both regard and respect because of its influence upon other faiths. Some Christian writers have even given it the credit of remoulding Hebrew beliefs and practices. Lessing compares the experiences of Israel under the Persians to that of a child who goes from home and finds that other children

[1] Dr. Muir's *Sanskrit Texts*, vol. iii. p. 180.

know more than himself;[1] but the undoubted
change effected during the captivity would be
more fittingly ascribed to the discipline of the
exile, which was foretold as what would bring
about national religious reform (Deut. xxvii.,
xxx.).   There is much that is attractive in the
noble creed of the Avesta, which is said to be
only a fragment of the sacred books of the Parsis,
the rest having been burned or lost in troublous
times.   In several respects it comes nearer to the
Bible, as claiming revelation, than any other non-
biblical religion, with the exception of Moham-
medanism.   But even when we find it stated that
Ormazd (or the good god) revealed certain
things to Zarathustra (Zoroaster), we have to
notice how the revelation betrays its human
origin by stating, with unvarying repetition, that
man always asked the question, and that the
revelation was God's answer.   This is little like
the Bible, where we see how God sought out

[1] Lessing says of the experience of Israel under the Persians: 'As
yet the Jewish people had reverenced in their Jehovah rather the
mightiest than the wisest of all gods; as yet they had rather feared
Him as a jealous God than loved Him. . . . [But now] Instead of, as
hitherto, appreciating Him in contrast with the miserable idols of the
small neighbouring peoples with whom they lived in constant rivalry,
they began, in captivity under the wise Persians, to measure Him
against the "Being of all Beings," such as a more disciplined reason
recognised and reverenced. . . . Since the Jews by this time, through
the medium of the pure Persian doctrine, recognised in their Jehovah
not simply the greatest of all national deities, but God. etc.'—*Education
of the Human Race*, §§ 34, 35, 39.   For a similar, and, I believe, exaggerated view of the power and value of Zoroastrianism, see Milne's Lecture
in *Faiths of the World: St. Giles' Lectures*, 2d series.

man, and lifted him up, and sustained him, and taught him to desire and to hope, and trained him and prepared him, till in the fulness of time the Saviour was sent to unite him with God for ever. This also has to be noticed, that the myths of the Avesta are either derived from the myths of the Veda, or from an older source, which was also the parent of the Vedic religion, and that the Vedic hymns themselves, which are far older than the Avesta, do not, as we have seen, claim to be a revelation, so that the later religion, which is the child or the younger brother of Brahmanism, can scarcely make such a claim with success.[1] Even if it made such a claim, its mean view of God's holiness, its inadequate estimate of man's depravity, its often degrading and never more than human requirements intimated to man in order that he may attain to holiness, its frequently filthy ritual (even though it be more concerned with cleanliness than with holiness), would combine to show how unable it is to bear close comparison with the Old Testament, not to speak of the New.[2]

When Brahmanism had degenerated into an

---

[1] See Darmesteter's *Transl. of the Zend Avesta*, *Fargards* xviii. and xix., and Introduction, § 41. Also Haug's *Essays on the Language, Writings, and Religion of the Parsis*. 'The Zoroastrian religion arose out of a vital struggle against the form which the Brahmanical religion had assumed at a certain early period.'

[2] See this sharply brought out in Dr. John Wilson's *Parsi Religion, as contained in the Zend Avesta*.

empty ceremonial, and men's minds were burdened
with the gods many and lords many of the ancient
creed of India, Sakya Muni, the enlightened sage,
—the Buddha,—arose and made a great revolt.
He preached a pure life, a life of pity and of
love; he had no patience with the piety that was
invoking idols for help to oneself, when the sick
and the sorrowful, and the poor of our human
brotherhood, are in need at our door and at our
hand.   The religion which he founded, which
holds in its thrall one-third of the human race,
has greatly changed since its founder lived under
the Bo Tree, or with his few disciples preached
the religion of self-denial for others' sake, and the
extirpation of all passions.   It has now legends
attached to its great founder's name, and it has
books in abundance; but a religion which neither
recognised God nor soul, though it probably
denied neither, cannot claim to be founded on
revelation,[1] and it does not therefore compare
with Judaism or with Christianity.

Of the only remaining religion—Mohammedan-
ism—it is not necessary to speak.   Its claim to
be a revelation is undoubted; but it is so
obviously a barefaced imitation of the Bible—
both of the Old Testament and of the New—
that we need not tarry over it.   Though it con-

---

[1] The main objections of Brahmans to it are that it is not a revelation.
See Müller, *Hist. of Sansk. Lit.* p. 81.

tains great and salutary truths regarding God, they are obviously taken from our Scriptures.[1] It remains, however, the only religion outside of the Bible which claims beyond doubt to have been a revelation from God.

Our hasty survey has given us ground for doubting the sweeping statement of Professor Max Müller, which, though in guarded phrase, undoubtedly suggests that all religions claim, as Judaism and Christianity claim, to arise from a divine revelation. As a matter of fact, we see that none of the books of other religions — save the Mohammedan Koran—make a claim that can be said to be parallel to that of the Bible.

But while we think there may be vindicated for the Bible the existence of a claim which, both in kind and in degree, is special to it, we are well aware that the existence of such a claim is not tantamount to its establishment. What we have said to-night bears only on the amount of acceptance demanded by the Bible from those who accept it, and establishes this conclusion at least, that any mere expression of respect for the good intentions, or for the ability, or for the high

---

[1] Mohammed at first was content to identify his religion with Judaism and Christianity. He often speaks of Moses as the man, and Israel as the people, to whom 'God gave the Book.' In his later times he attempted to justify his position—and his immoralities—by new and special revelations; but even in them he was an imitator of the Bible. See *Suras* xxxi., xlv., xlvi., lvii. See Sir W. Muir's *The Koran*, and Dr. Marcus Dods' *Mahomet, Buddha, and Christ*.

intuition of its various writers, will not satisfy its
imperious demand. It claims to stand alone in its
authoritative position as the word of the living and
true God. Its voice still is: 'To you, O men,—
all men,—I call.' 'God hath spoken to you by
His Son.' 'The gospel is come to you, as unto
all the world;' and upon every one who hears
there is laid the old and ever new obligation to
go and teach all nations, baptizing them into the
name of the Father, and of the Son, and of the
Holy Ghost. It will not be put off with deference or with respect when obedience is demanded.

But this does not mean that the Bible should
be shielded by its believers from examination or
inquiry. To make any attempt at shielding our
sacred books would of course be vain. These are
no times to keep a holy thing in some sanctuary,
where only an official or a believer can search or
know it. But, moreover, if in our most secret
thoughts we had any idea that such shielding
were even desirable, we should be in God's sight
the enemies of His truth. 'I speak as to wise
men, judge ye what I say' (1 Cor. x. 15), said
the fearless and frank apostle. 'I think myself
happy that I am to make my defence before thee
this day' (Acts xxvi. 2), were his words when
called to expound his gospel to one who may be
described as an educated sceptic.

Modern questioning requires to be met in the

same spirit. There are indeed some of the ques-
tioners who arrogate to themselves a monopoly
of the title of honest inquirers, and who, with
curiously suicidal dogmatism, assume that all
whose position is one of confident belief must have
lacked either ability to inquire or honesty to avow
the inevitable conclusion. There are probably some
others who are moved by a conscious desire to find
Christianity untrue, who love darkness rather than
light because their deeds are evil. But there
are others, and many of them, who are earnestly
examining the very foundations of the Christian
faith, and who would undoubtedly be glad to have
assurance that it is true; for they desire nothing
better than to walk in the truth. And there are
others among ourselves who, never having searched
into the principles of the things they most surely
believe, are unable to encounter those who subject
the Christian books to the same kind of test as
our missionaries and others who meet Moham-
medans, or Hindus, or Chinese, apply to the
sacred books of the faiths of the East. I believe
with all my heart that the New Testament can
bear the fiercest light of modern investigation.
I believe that the unparalleled vigour of the
critical assaults which have been made upon it
since the nineteenth century began, have not
brought down a single tower of its citadel. And
I therefore believe that the inquiry on which we

C

are entering will not end without our seeing good grounds for granting the claim of our sacred books to be regarded as canonical,—that is to say, they will be seen to be the words of Him who said: 'The words which I speak unto you, they are spirit, and they are life' (John vi. 63). This can only be true if the Spirit quickens them. May He come to us each and every one!

LECTURE II.

WE now endeavour to pursue the inquiry into the characteristics of those Scriptures which claim truth, unity, and authority.

And we have to remark—1. *That while the Scriptures claim to be the Word of God, given by inspiration of His Spirit, they do not enable us to ascertain the nature or the extent of inspiration.* It is quite true that, speaking of the Old Testament, St. Paul ascribes inspiration to the Scriptures. But in the words of St. Paul we have, first of all, a grammatical difficulty illustrated by our Authorized Version as compared with that of the recent Revisers. The words may mean, as in the Authorized Version, 'All Scripture is given by inspiration of God, and is profitable,' or, as in the Revised Version, 'Every Scripture inspired of God is also profitable.' There being no substantive verb [is] in the original, we are left to supply it where it may seem best. And the grammatical difficulty which thus arises as to its proper place is illustrated by those two renderings in our own tongue. But even if it be pleaded, as it may well be, that, when taken in connection with the context, the words in either case mean to claim for all the sacred writings, which Timothy had known from his childhood, at once inspiration and such profitableness as to make the man of God completely furnished unto every good work, there still remains the difficulty of interpretation. It centres in the Greek adjective translated 'given by inspiration of God,' or 'inspired of God.' It is a great word, an invaluable word. It claims for all the Bible known to Timothy that the Supreme Spirit breathed it. But when we try to realize what this means, we find that the knowledge is too high for us. The word is a lock, not a key. What does it mean? We must find the answer in Scripture. Other Scriptures may explain it, but it certainly does not explain the other Scriptures.

But do other Scriptures explain it? Do they tell us what in every case was meant by speaking or writing words which were 'breathed of God'? I think not. It has not been uncommon to attempt to distinguish between the different degrees of inspiration, and to write upon the inspiration of suggestion, or of superintendence, or of dictation. This distinction has been derived from the Jews, who carried it out so thoroughly as to ascribe different degrees of authority to the various

sections of their Bible on the ground of their
resulting from various grades of inspiration. They
anticipated many critics of our own day in attempting to arrange the holy writings according to their
supposed importance. When they asked the new
Rabbi what was in his opinion the great commandment of the law, they sought to make him take a
side in their controversies of this kind. Their
threefold division of the Bible encouraged them
in this : Moses and the law ranking high above
the others ; for Moses, they said, was made par-
taker of divine revelations with open, wakeful eye
looking direct on God, to whom he could at all
times refer (Num. vii. 89), while to all other prophets
were sent dreams or visions or angelic messengers,
so that they were not in their natural state, but in
an astonied or rapt condition, when the breath of
the Spirit came upon them.

In the same way Matthew Arnold, in his many
beautifully verbose books, tells us at once what
is the essential portion of any part of Scripture ;
what was St. Paul's original meaning in some of
his doctrines (say of Resurrection, see p. 83 of *St.
Paul and Protestantism*), and how he grew out of
any physical meaning of the phrases he used,
spiritualizing them altogether, though he himself
never understood how he had changed, which,
however, Mr. Arnold happily explains for him ;
and how most unhappily 'Paul was led into diffi-

culty by the tendency [which we have already noticed as] making his real imperfection both as a thinker and as a ruler—the tendency to Judaize.'

All this means that Mr. Arnold has decided what true Christianity is, apart from St. Paul, and proceeds to adjust the apostle to himself, flouting the great Christian teacher at last when his words will not bend in the critic's deft handling.

The world moves in circles, and the traditions and theories which are buried for generations re-appear in the conflicts of some subsequent time. There are many whose various theories are only applications of their principle that the degree of the inspiration, and therefore of the authority or the importance of any part of Scripture, is to be ascertained by estimating the amount of its insight into the essence of Christianity. We may take a living theologian for example. 'The importance of any particular part of the Bible depends,' says Schenkel, 'on the closeness of its relation to Christ.' He goes on to say that the highest place is occupied by the Gospels, the highest rank among the Gospels belonging to that of St. John. In the second rank stand the Apostolical Epistles; those of St. Paul and St. John standing before those of St. Peter, and these, again, before those of St. James and St. Jude. In the third rank comes the Apocalypse. *'Scripture which has reference to Christ as the central point of the history of redemption*

is in its immediate divine origin the Word of God.
It is true both that Scripture is the Word of God,
and that the Word of God is in Scripture. On
the other hand, it is an error, and in the highest
degree misleading, to regard each single utterance
or isolated text of Scripture as the Word of God.'[1]

We might well pause before adopting theories
which are chargeable with the arrogance of assuming that the critic is a competent judge of the
amount of spiritual insight enjoyed by a writer
in the Bible. We might grant to him that books
when judged by their own claims will fall into
ranks, so that, for example, Proverbs would furnish no such utterance for the higher spiritual
emotions of man as the Psalms give, because the
Proverbs—even in the stately tenderness of the
opening chapters—are only meditations upon life
addressed to man, while the Psalms are divinely
prompted words ascending to God. So, too, the
Epistle of James is not intelligible in itself, and
requires as a basis such a revelation of the life
and words of Christ as we find in the Gospels.
It is of its nature supplementary, just as the book
of Proverbs is. But that is quite another thing
from our proceeding to cut Scripture into pieces
according to what we believe to be the amount
of spiritual insight which it shows. Moreover, to

[1] See *Inspiration*, by a Layman [Dr. John Muir], with a Preface by
H. B. Wilson, p. 234.

all such theories, whatever modification they may
assume, one fatal objection applies. They are not
based upon Scripture itself. They are an evolution from human consciousness; and they are
impelled by a baseless idea that it is needful to
have some theory of the grades of inspiration.
There is not in Scripture any trace of one writer
subordinating himself to another. There is no
authority there for one man setting John above
all the rest, and another setting Paul or Peter.
The Divine Spirit hath spoken 'by diverse
portions and in divers manners,' that all the
diversities of the human family may find some
portion specially adapted to them. Strength for
the strong, and 'pleadings for the shame and
feebleness' of them that have no might; heroic
deeds to stir the souls of the young and ardent;
spiritual musings to suffuse the spirit of the meditative: to each one of His children the Great
Father on whom wait all their eyes gives meat
in due season (Ps. cxlv. 15). The revealing and
redeeming Son has told us which is the first and
great commandment of the ancient law, and of all
the laws that have ever come from God, and He
has told us that to know the true God and Jesus
Christ whom He hath sent is eternal life; but
He did not come to establish a hierarchy of
inspiration in His Church. We cannot and dare
not say that there were not various degrees of

force and fulness in the effusion of the Holy Spirit in ancient or in modern times. We may believe that the delivery of the Decalogue stood by itself a direct objective revelation to man, not through any other man; but we do most strenuously affirm that there is no warrant in the Bible for attempting to grade the inspiration of those whose writings compose it, or to define the nature of the influence under which they wrote. Unless from the divine side, it is impossible that such a gradation can be made; and on the divine side who shall take his stand? On the human side all the writers claim truth, unity, and authority.

It is wonderful how little we learn from Scripture itself as to the way in which truth was made known. 'By angelic appearances, dreams, visions, ecstasy, voices from heaven, and symbolic acts,' the divine thoughts were conveyed to men.[1] Sometimes also there seems to have come, as from within the mind, a divine impulse that carried the prophet before it (Num. xxiii. 5, 20, but comp. xxiv. 4).[2] The variety of modes is very great, but the result is the same. 'No prophecy ever came by the will of man; but men spake from God, being moved by the Holy Ghost' (2 Pet. i. 21).

---

[1] Lee on *Inspiration*, p. 113.
[2] 'Like the Midianite of old,
    Who stood on Zophim heaven-controlled,
    I feel within mine aged breast
    A power that will not be repressed.'— *Walter Scott.*

2. *This being so, it is vain to hold that we are under any necessity to have some theory of inspiration.* It is vain, because we cannot hope to make bricks without straw. We cannot build up a doctrine when God has not revealed it. It is under the influence of a false idea of the necessity of some theory of inspiration that so many have tried to adjust the facts to the theory which gained their support.

This is obvious if we ask to what inspiration amounted? what was the effect of it upon the resulting Word? There is much to be said, on the one hand, for the position of those who hold that Scripture, if it be the Word of God, must have been absolutely and unalterably true in every word, syllable, and letter as it was first given to and by the inspired men. If any portion of the revealing Word be erroneous, say they, so may all; and thus we have no word of prophecy whereunto we do well to take heed. If the true theory be that the Bible contains the Word of God,—not that the Bible is the Word of God,—then who is to settle how much is shell and what is kernel? how deep is the rind to be peeled off ere we reach the divine core of the revelation?

But there is much also to be said for those who plead, on the other hand, that so stringent a theory leads into unnecessary difficulties, making the strength of the chain not greater than that of its

weakest link, and so destroying all the power of
Scripture if even one error can be made manifest
in any portion of the Canon, however subsidi-
ary. They hold that it is not in every detail,
but in the whole scope of the Scripture, we shall
find the revelation by which to live. They say
that this is according to the analogy of the divine
procedure. God reveals Himself in His works so
clearly that an honest mind can be convinced of
His infinite power and Godhead; but yet not so
as that the enemy has never marred the revelation
—not so as that everything which happens in the
world is surely a representation of God. The
human passions are not the image of the holy
God; decay and death are not necessary concomi-
tants of life; errors are not necessary parts of
thought. All these, which actually exist, are in
themselves interruptions of the revelation of God
written in humanity and in providence as a whole;
and yet over all, and in all, and through all, God
works, causing all things to work together for good
to them that love Him, making the very wrath of
the wicked to praise Him. If to all this we reply
that the Word of God is given for the very purpose
of guiding us unerringly through the perplexities
of life, so that if it be itself mixed with error, or
even if error clouds it, we have no guide, the
rejoinder readily comes. It is an argument from
analogy, from the spiritual experience of God's

children. It is to the effect that God's Spirit is
the author of all true life, the prompter of every
holy thought and purpose; yet not so that we can
always distinguish God's Spirit from our own in
any mental state into which we may come, nor
even so that we can always be sure that fancy or
human enthusiasm is not conjoined in our soul with
the pure suggestions of the Spirit of God. But
notwithstanding all such occasional uncertainty,
causing us to walk warily and to examine our
own selves, there is undoubtedly a Spirit coming
from God, according to His promise. Again,
therefore, they ask whether the analogy may not
hold in the written Word which the same Spirit
gave; whether it may not be our duty, the very
exercise of our responsibility, to distinguish in
Scripture the human from the divine, the temporary from the everlasting. They give up the
idea of perfect freedom from error in every minute
matter; but they own no error in the Scripture as
a whole, which they believe to be the very word of
the living God.[1] They do not succeed in making
it clear to others that they regard the revelation
of God in the Bible as the authoritative standard,
—for it seems to many that the 'inner light'
which they have is really their supreme authority,

---

[1] 'We do not possess a Canon that is absolutely free from mistake,
nor, indeed, do we require it. What we require is a record of revelation absolutely true, and that we possess in the Scriptures' (Auberlen on
Divine Revelation, p. 242).

—but they themselves declare that the 'inner light' has been awakened and *is regulated* by the Spirit speaking through the written Word, so that the Word is the standard, and the light within them is the application to them of that standard by the Spirit of God, who gave it at the first.

There is much to be said on both sides; and within the limits which I have endeavoured to indicate, I do not see why good men may not agree to differ. We learn from those whose position I have last described, that life being higher than logic, we shall do ill to reproduce the weakness of the creeds of the Reformed Churches, which try to map out all the nature and work of God according to logical inferences from intellectual statements; and that it well beseems us to admit the possibility of a truth of intuition which does not come as the last step in a syllogism. We learn from the other side that there is no small danger in being dogmatically undogmatical in declaring that a book is true as a whole, while in every detail, great and small, it is liable to error. Errors, as a matter of fact, are admitted by good men on all sides to exist in the books as we now have them, due in most cases to the slips of copyists, but yet such that we have no means of removing them. The fact that good men on both sides admit the existence of such errors, and yet maintain the supreme authority of Scripture, may

warn us to beware of dogmatism on either side.
It may teach us to shrink from the fierce consistency of the advocates of verbal dictation, without driving us to manifest the arrogance of those
who cut and carve in Holy Writ as they think
fit,—as though their own minds were the highest
of all revelation,—as though they were sure of
this one thing only, that there is neither miracle
nor marvel in the collection of documents which
have 'turned the world upside down.'

Instead of indulging in vain speculations, let us
proceed inductively to search the Scriptures, that
we may attain to certain principles that will regu-
late our use of our holy books. Those principles
will, as it seems to me, enable us to hold intelligently by the validity of the claims to authority
advanced in Scripture. And in thus proceeding
we remark that—

3. *Something higher than ordinary honesty and
accuracy must be ascribed to the writers of Scripture if their writings are to be accepted at all.*
Many tell us to judge Scripture as we judge any
other book. But if we do so, and admit its
accuracy, we set it where no other book can be
set. The prophets profess to predict future events.
This statement involves either much more or much
less than ordinary historical trustworthiness,—much
more if the words were really predictions, much less
if they were written after the event, and falsely

passed off as predictions. This is true of the New Testament as well as of the Old. The fall of Jerusalem as foretold by Jesus Christ, the relation of the fate of Israel to the ingathering of the Gentiles as announced by St. Paul to the Romans, are not to be disposed of as ordinary statements of a historical character.

Nor only this. If we accept the disciples as veracious reporters or annalists, who truly tell what things they saw and heard, then they had higher gifts than mere veracity, because they claimed to have the Holy Ghost. The Comforter, who came after Christ's death, is said to have inspired the followers of Christ, enabling them to understand His life and teachings, and guiding them into all the truth (John xvi. 13). If, then, this were true, the apostles were more than ordinary historians. They were inspired men, speaking of what they had been supernaturally enabled to understand and declare.

4. *We cannot say that Scripture in any part is only divine, or, on the other hand, that it is only human.* The attempt, which was at one time common enough, to speak of Scripture as though it had been dictated by the Holy Ghost to men passively receiving the inspiration and transmitting the truth to others, as some lifeless mechanical instrument might, is now universally abandoned. It is felt to be unnecessary. God, who searcheth the heart

and trieth the reins, can speak through His creature by using that creature's special characteristics ; and even if the Word were wholly His, it might naturally bear the marks of the human speaker as well. The truth would still be wholly God's, whether spoken in a loud voice or in a whisper, whether by lordly Isaiah or by Amos the herdsman. And the theory is more than unnecessary—it is false to the facts. It is inconsistent with the exuberance and the variety of life which mark Holy Scripture. The idiosyncrasies of different authors come out as clearly in the Bible as in any other book. The Gospels are four pictures of Christ taken from four distinct standpoints ; and since Christians began interpreting, it has been the delight of interpreters to regard each of the four writers as symbolized by one of the four living creatures of the ancient vision of Ezekiel. The eagle, the lion, the sacrificial ox, and the man have been accepted as the symbols of the cherubim whose 'faces were the images of the dispensation of the Son of God' (Irenæus, iii. 11, 8).[1]

When we read the Old and New Testaments we can as easily understand from their own writings

---

[1] Irenæus reasons that as there are four winds, four zones, so there must be four gospels to make the dispensation complete. He assigns the lion to John, the fatted calf to Luke, the man to Matthew, and the eagle to Mark. But in later times most writers follow Jerome and Augustine in referring the 'eagle' to John, the 'ox' to Luke, Jerome assigning the 'man' to Matthew and the 'lion' to Mark, while Augustine (less rightly) reverses this allocation.

the differences of character in Peter and Paul and James and John, in Isaiah, Jeremiah, and Daniel, as in Herodotus and Thucydides, in Tacitus and Livy. The human elements are too obvious to be overlooked.

But equally so are the divine. Future events were foretold and a coming redemption prefigured, things beyond the ken of mortal man were declared, all witnessing for God through the Spirit, all showing that the Supreme Author of the book is God Himself. The New Testament gives us a formula by which to express the truth : David said in the Holy Spirit, or, Well spake the Holy Ghost through Esaias. We see sometimes the divine, sometimes the human, put more prominently when the New Testament is citing the Old. Thus the same passage in Isaiah which tells of the hardening of the heart of Israel so that it could not receive the truth is quoted by St. John (xii. 41) with the words : ' These things said Isaiah ;' while St. Paul, speaking to the Jews in Rome, says : ' Well spake the Holy Ghost by Isaiah unto your fathers.' So also St. Matthew writes that Christ on one occasion quoted the Fifth Commandment, saying : ' For God commanded ' (Matt. xv. 4) ; while in the parallel narrative of St. Mark we read : ' For Moses said, Honour thy father and thy mother.'[1]

---

[1] We find in the use made of the Old Testament in the New many significant facts. There are 275 passages of the New Testament which

We cannot ' redd the marches ' between the human and the divine in Holy Scripture. Θεῖα πάντα καὶ ἀνθρώπινα πάντα.[1]

5. *Passing from the subject of inspiration to that of revelation, we find that no promise is made that all the words of Jesus or of His apostles would be infallibly and miraculously preserved.* On the contrary, John tells us that the world

are considered as quotations from the Old. Of these, 65 agree with the original Hebrew; 37 agree with the LXX., but not with the Hebrew; 99 differ from both, they also differing from each other; 77 differ from both, they agreeing with each other. There are three other passages—John vii. 38, vii. 42, and Eph. v. 14—which are obviously not meant to be quotations, but condensations of or allusions to several well-known passages of Scripture. (The fullest and most careful information on this subject is to be found in Dr. M'Calman Turpie's *Old Testament in the New.*) In many of those quotations in the New Testament the changes made on the Old Testament are very slight, not amounting to more than the omission or transposition of a word. The general tenor of the New Testament is that it rests upon or grows out of the Old Testament. See Rom. iii. 10 for an appeal to the authority of five texts of the Old Testament combined, or Mark i. 2 for an illustration drawn from Mal. iii. 1, combined with Isaiah xl. 3. See the meaning of Gen. ii. 24 developed and made more emphatic in Matt. xix. 5. Compare 1 Cor. vi. 16, Eph. v. 31. These are proofs of freedom in the use of the Old Testament, and imply on the part of the New Testament writers a right to deal freely, a right drawn from the same authority as that which gave the Word at the first. But again, lest we should use the Old Testament too freely, we must note that stress is laid upon the very words of the Old Testament (Matt. xxii. 32; Gal. iii. 16).

[1] Mr. Stopford Brooke, who says that it is ' no longer in his power to believe in the miraculous foundation of Christianity,' and that he has left the Church of England 'not to be less but to be more of a Christian,' proceeds with an uneasy audacity that is in many ways pathetic to justify his step by diminishing the authority of the New Testament books. He will tell you as to a chapter in the Apocalypse where the seer was ' writing prosaically,' with ' nothing but the old Judaic thought ' in what he says, and where that seer began to write by inspiration. And then, lest we should too much defer to John, he hastens to add that ' inspiration belongs to all of us, . . . is the right and privilege of every man and woman ' (*Spirit of the Christian Life*, pp. 242–244).

would not contain all the books which would be written were the record of Christ's life full. No one can for a moment suppose that the Hebrew Canon contains all the inspired words of the prophets whom Jehovah sent to Israel, 'rising up early' to send them. Nor of Jesus Himself, or of His apostles, are the spoken words recorded save to a small extent. It is unwarrantable to suppose that all which was of permanent application remains, while that which has perished was only for the time and place of speaking. There is absolutely no trace of authority for such a statement.

It is equally unwarrantable to suppose, à priori, that all the Christian writings of permanent value have been preserved. Though there is no absolutely cogent proof, there is some reason to believe that one of Paul's letters to the Corinthians is lost.

It is scarcely possible to imagine that those two short letters of the aged John are all that he wrote to his friends when he alone survived of those who had been with the Lord in the flesh.

And if God were miraculously to preserve a writing, He would surely miraculously preserve each part of it. In that case, there would be no various readings in the sacred books which survive through the centuries. There must be, in our own time, some one copy of the text to which we can always refer as an infallible standard by which disputes must be decided. But that it is not so,—that human reason and loving care are well employed in searching which of many forms is likely to have been the original clothing of some divine truth,—our everyday experience amply proves.

But we must nevertheless observe the wonderfully designed adaptation of circumstances to holy ends in the whole history of the sacred writings. In the case of the Old Testament, continual instruction in the words of Scripture, and the multiplication of copies that such instruction might be given in all the lands of the Dispersion, furnished a safeguard for the immutableness of the record. The extraordinary, even superstitious, value attached by the Jews to the minutest jot and tittle of their books was a further protection to it. And accordingly, when we find that the strange people retain as their Bible a series of prophecies, which they are at their wits' end to interpret of any other than Jesus of Nazareth, yet which they have not altered or abridged through all the centuries, we see the providence of God, though we may not call it an infallible miracle.[1]

[1] On this subject Harnack (see Brieger's *Zeitschrift* for 1879, pp. 358 ff. and 596 ff.) tries to draw some remarkable conclusions from the innocent phrases of the Muratorian Fragment. He thinks that 'Paul's Epistles may not yet have been read in many congregations in the first half of the second century, though' [he naïvely adds] 'proofs of it are wanting'! There is 'no trace of hostility to Paul on the part of

The same is true of the New Testament. Paul's Epistles were read in the various churches of Christendom even while the apostle lived; and they were soon known to all the scattered children of God, so that their hard sayings were familiar (2 Peter iii. 16). Thus early, therefore, the reverence of Christians throughout the world for the writings of the apostles furnished a guarantee that those writings would be preserved without essential change or material loss.[1] Save that the whole dispensation is miraculous, and that the Church has in it the abiding miracle of the presence of Christ by His Spirit, we cannot call this special providence a miracle. But it is a proof of the 'singular care and providence of God.'

I may here use the calculation and illustration of an eminent American critic (Professor Norton). Gibbon estimates that the population of the Roman Empire in the time of the Antonines was about 120,000,000, and that not more than one-twentieth of the whole were Christian before the conversion of Constantine. This seems an

the author of the Fragment;' but he says, 'I can only account for the fact by the supposition that the public reading of the Pauline letters in the congregations never ceased, notwithstanding the ignoring of the actual Paul, and was established in far the majority of churches.' It would not occur to any one but an ingenious critic as possible to read the letters of Paul and ignore the actual Paul. Yet this is the keystone of a new theory which is intended to supplant or complement that of Baur.

[1] See Newman's *Grammar of Assent* for testimonies, p. 468.

inadequate estimate, for when the first century closed Pliny found that 'the contagion of this superstition had made its way not in cities only, but in the lesser towns also, and in the open country.' A hundred years later (about A.D. 200), Tertullian said : 'We are but of yesterday, and we have filled everything that is yours : cities, islands, castles, factories, council halls, the very camps, all classes of men, the palace, the city, the forum. We have left you nothing but your temples. We can number your armies ; there are more Christians in a single province. . . . If we, such a multitude of men, had broken away from you, retiring into some remote corner of the world, your government would have been covered with shame at the loss of so many citizens, whoever they might be. The very desertion would have punished you. Without doubt you would have been terrified at your solitude ; at the silence and stupor of all things, as if the world were dead. You would have had to look about for subjects.'

But let us grant that the Christians were about one-twentieth of the population of the empire at the end of the third century. Let us suppose that they were one-fortieth at the end of the second century. If so, we have at that date three millions of Christians. If we suppose that there was one copy of the Gospels for every fifty Christians,—a number as great as was likely to be found in one place of meeting,—we have sixty thousand copies in all in the year A.D. 200.[1]

This is a very large number, but it can seem incredible and improbable to none save those who know that books were scarce in the Middle Ages, and that they must have been scarcer in the days of the Antonines. The first three centuries of Christianity were times of far greater and more widely diffused intellectual and religious activity than those which followed. Men were more anxious in those early days to know the Christian records than they were afterwards, when the ecclesiastical and monastic systems were fully established. At that later time Greek was almost unknown in the Western monasteries, and the mass of men was illiterate. But at the beginning of the Christian era writing was a common accomplishment ; books —both in Greek and in Latin—were so much multiplied by shorthand writers and copyists as to be sold cheap. Bookselling was a large and flourishing trade in Rome, and it continued for long to increase in favour and popularity. If an ordinary copy of 272 verses of Martial could be had for a halfpenny (leaving a profit to the bookseller), and a luxurious copy of his Epigrams for fivepence, it is clear that literature was within the reach of most men.

The Christian community from the very first showed that it shared in the characteristics of a

---

[1] Norton, *Genuineness of the Gospels*, vol. ii. p. 32 ff.

literary time. We have frequent references to writing in the New Testament; both heathens and Christians habitually wrote. All Paul's friends wrote for him, and, as a rule, he only added a few salutations with his own hand to what his friends had written for him. Origen, the great scholar of the third century, had seven shorthand writers in his own employment, and many girls who wrote out fair copies. He says books were not confined to students, but were in most common use. It is in the multiplication of copies of the New Testament that we find the reason of so many various readings in small points, and also the complete security for no important error being allowed to exist. It is in this way also that we account for the loss of the originals of the New Testament writings, though they were preserved for a considerable time in the places to which they were first sent. The copies were so many, so good, and so universally circulated, that men ceased to refer to the originals as anything special, and the originals were used like the others and worn out. Thus we have no difficulty in believing that there were sixty thousand copies of the Gospels for the three millions of Christians.

6. *Assuming that the record of revelation in the Bible is preserved with substantial accuracy, we find in it the record of a progressive revelation.* We make no attempt to go beyond the limits

of the Bible narratives when we try to speak of
progress in religious knowledge.   There is not
much to tempt us to go beyond them if we would
deal with ascertained results.   Those who seek
to trace the steps of man's progress in religion
without revelation are not agreed either as to the
point at which it began, or as to the stages by
which it advanced.   Some—following (or accom-
modating) the great high priest of Positivism—
would have us believe that all religion began
with fetich-worship, *i.e.* the worship of natural
objects or their emblems ; others would have it
that the first step was the worship of the sky ;
others find it in the worship of the spirits of
deceased ancestors ; but there is no agreement
as to the initial point, nor as to what succeeded.
The sun shines at the present day on tribes and
nations of men practising all those forms of
idolatry, but the study of human nature and of
human speech cannot decide whether the lowest
form is a beginning of upward progress, or is only
the latest result of a long process of degradation.
Men of science must give up the attempt to
account, on material or rationalistic grounds, for
that sense of the supernatural which dominates
man ; no number of supposed stages can make it
easy to understand when or how man began the
process in course of which he has come to worship
One God, the Spirit.   They will have at last to

seek shelter in an older and simpler creed than any of those compromises with 'Positivism' which are so current. 'There is a spirit in man, and the inspiration of the Almighty giveth him understanding;' and that spirit witnesses to the being and power of the Spiritual God. Religion is not man-made, though it has been perverted and degraded by man. It is not so philosophical to hold what Max Müller seems to hold,—that Monotheism is a refinement upon Polytheism, that the idea of deity grew out of the previous ideas of many supernatural powers, so 'that the predicate "God," which is looked for and slowly conquered, that the intuition of the divine, is by its very nature one,'[1]—as to hold with Lessing that idolatry was the degradation of primitive Monotheism, a degradation which came because 'the human reason left to itself broke up the Immeasurable into many measurables, and gave a note or sign of mark to every one of these parts.'[2]

Nor on grounds of abstract philosophy alone is this true. Recent evidence goes to discredit Comte's idea that fetichism is the beginning of religion,[3] and

---

[1] *Hibbert Lectures*, p. 273.

[2] *Education of the Human Race*, § 6.

[3] Fetichism is a term due to De Brosses in his book *Les Dieux Fétiches* (1760). He also invented the words 'Australia' and 'Polynesia.' *Feitiços* = factitious (something made), was the word by which Portuguese sailors designated the charms or amulets which they wore. Africans used also charms (*gri-gris*), and ascribed to them magical virtues, and the sailors called them also *fétiches*. But the savage invests his fetich, just as the Roman Catholic does, with powers

to exhibit fetichism as a corruption of something better. This is true of Polytheism also. The great trouble in the way of those who regard religion as man-made is the necessity of accounting for its existence. Whence came the sense of the super-natural? Why did man feel after God if haply he might find Him? It might be that in this endea-vour of feeling, man advanced from the belief of many gods to the sublime worship of One; but how did man come to believe in many gods? That all the universe around him is pervaded by the spiritual and supernatural presence of Deity is the truth at the basis of even Polytheism; and how did man attain to the conviction of that truth? Before man could spread out an acknow-ledgment of Deity till it covered a whole Pan-theon, he must have been possessed of the faith which dictates that acknowledgment; and whence did it come? How did it begin?

It does not seem as though students of com-parative religion always duly estimate this diffi-culty. Nor does it seem clear that they have settled with themselves whether God is an inven-tion or a discovery; whether He exists or no.[1] Some say that religion is man-made; but do they

_____

of a supernatural kind—makes it a symbol, in short. But a symbol of what? Of something supernatural; the idea of which precedes the use of the symbol, and cannot be derived from it.

[1] See this powerfully brought out by the Duke of Argyll, *Contemp. Review*, vol. xxxix., especially p. 665 ff.

mean that God is man-made? It does not lie within our subject to dwell upon what is called comparative religion; but it was needful to say thus much in explanation of our confining ourselves to the record given in the Bible.[1] In the present unsettled condition of the whole study no other course is possible. This, too, we may say, that the most recent inquiries and comparisons, by bringing out the fact of 'progress' in religion being so often downward, are going far to establish on scientific grounds the belief to which so many have clung, because they believe in the teaching of the Bible, that there was a primeval revela-

[1] Though Comte's notion of all religion beginning in fetichism—a natural basis for such a structure as his—is apparently discarded by most students, or held with modifications, there is still great unwillingness to exempt religion from the idea of progress upwards by evolution. Some suppose that they have found the key to the difficulty when they exalt Henotheism—whether the local supremacy of one god at each centre of population (as in Egypt), or the 'successive belief in single supreme gods' (as in the Vedas), be meant by the term. But, granting that Henotheism stands midway between Monotheism and Polytheism, there remains the old question as to the direction in which man's face was turned when his foot stood on this stepping-stone. Was he going up or down? If up—towards Monotheism—then (1) how did his ideas of the supernatural begin? and (2) how did they come to tend in this direction? Those questions are not answered. If a merely human view of religion—a view that it is man-made—be sought for, surely the best is that of those who hold that early heathen religions began in the worship of the sky, and that Polytheism was the next stage in what was originally a vague reverence for the power dwelling in the firmament. This is obviously a progress downward; and there is good reason for believing that this was the case. The idea of a great supreme god first; then the worship of the sky, and so on. Thus the doctrine of revelation is consistent with scientific study of the facts. See Poole's Essays in *Contemp. Review*, vol. xxxix., for many interesting facts. See Keary's *Outlines of Primitive Belief* for a modification of Comtism: Man worshipped the trees at his feet, and then rose to the sky and the Deity!

tion, of which all heathenism is a corruption ; that
'God made man upright, but that he has sought
out many inventions.'

But let us turn to the Bible itself.   We do
not find a progress in unbroken order as regards
some aspects of truth.   It is of the earliest age
of man we are told that Enoch walked with God,
and that Abraham was the friend of God.   The
personal presence of God could not be more distinctly felt by any of their posterity.   As regards
an individual's own sanctified life, I do not see
any proof that an Israelite was more advanced
than an antediluvian may have been, or than
Abraham was.   There seems to have been no
greater faith at any subsequent period than that
which was 'reckoned for righteousness' to the
father of the faithful.   The Mosaic polity was indispensable for the formation of a nation, and therefore it was given, but I do not know any respect
in which it was better for individuals.   But
there is an indubitable progress in man's understanding of the purposes of God in Christ
between the first dim expectation of the banished
pair, to which Eve bore pathetic witness when she
hailed her first-born, saying : 'I have gotten the
man from the Lord,' and that which David had
when he wrote the 110th Psalm :

'The Lord said unto my Lord,
Sit Thou at my right hand ; '

or that which Isaiah had when he said of the
Messiah : ' He bare the sin of many, and made
intercession for the transgressors.' So, too, we see
progress in regard to the prophetic aspects of
Christ's work between Moses' prediction of a
prophet like unto him and Malachi's announcement of the day of the Lord, for which one in the
spirit and power of Elias would prepare.

In the New Testament, also, we see a progress
in men's views not only during Christ's life, but
also after his death.   Pentecost itself did not
complete the preparation of the mind of the
disciples for the full width of Christian freedom ;
and we see, for example, both a widening and a
deepening in Peter's experience at Joppa, and at
the Council of Jerusalem (Acts xv.).   Paul himself was unwillingly turned by his experience of
facts, under divine guidance, from his chosen field
of Israel to become the apostle of the Gentiles.

In estimating the progress of this understanding,
it has always to be noted that each stage of progress was the result of a new revelation of which
men were conscious.   God, who had spoken to
the fathers, spoke again to them.   Daniel was
doubtless not the only one in the studious circles
of Israel, or of the exile, who ' understood by
the books ' some of the things which had been
spoken before ; but it was not by his study, but
by the revelation he was privileged to receive,

that Daniel added to the sacred roll of prophecy.
Each step—Sinai, the Temple, the Prophecies, the
Gospels, the Epistles—claims to be founded on a
special revelation.   The progress of which the
Bible speaks is not such as we might make, or
such as thoughtful and spiritual men might have
made at any time by dint of using the revelation
already in their hands.   It was not 'a predicate
looked for and slowly conquered' by inquiring
and resolute men.   In short, it is not progress in
interpretation but progress in revelation.   It is
true that greater progress in spiritual life and in
intelligent service might have been made if the
children of Israel had made the most of the
privileges they enjoyed.   The disciples were
charged by Jesus Himself with being fools and
slow of heart to believe all that the prophets had
written (Luke xxiv. 25, 44); and Paul, in like
manner, tells of the vail upon the hearts of Israel
when Moses is read (2 Cor. iii. 15); but still it
was not merely a right use of the old which
brought the new; it was the special interposition
of God, and the new revelation contained in His
incarnate life, that added to the ancient prophetic
Word, and took away the vail between Moses and
the Hebrew heart.   The unity of Scripture lies
not only in the progress being always in the same
direct line, but in each stage of it taking up
the unfinished work and the unsatisfied longings

of the stage which preceded (2 Peter i. 10, 11).
Abraham's family expected to be a nation, and
the nation was formed by Moses ; the people of
Israel expected in the time of Moses to have
united worship, a priesthood, and a line of
prophets, and these all came about as the scroll
of history was unrolled ; ritual, law, and prophecy
prefigured the Messiah, and with the fulness of
the times He came.   There is not in the New
Testament any ground to expect a similar further
development of the revelation ; the work of the
Spirit of Christ has still infinite progress to effect
that all nations may be made disciples, but we
are not led to expect a further addition to the
written Word.   God hath spoken to us by His
Son ; what need have we of further witness ?

In this arises one of the most difficult questions
in our Christian ethics : How far are the earlier
revelations a binding rule for those who live
under the later ?   But it seems as though the
difficulty were solved when we remember that
the dispensation under which we live is our only
rule.   The Old Testament is unto us a divine
book ; but we live under the gospel of Jesus
Christ ; and only in so far as the earlier revelation is adopted and confirmed by the gospel is it
in any degree binding upon us.   I know no doctrine of our faith which we are left to prove
from the Old Testament ; though the things

written aforetime were written for our learning,
that we might better understand the ways of
God in the revealing and redeeming life of His
Son. But when of all that work He could say
' It is finished,' that which is imperfect was done
away as a rule or standard. We are to explain
the Old Testament by the New, not the New by
the Old.

But this does not warrant any one to put aside
the early records as though they were untrue to
fact. No more are they falsified by being superseded than John the Baptist was. John must
decrease, the Christ must increase, because it is
He that should come. But that proves the truth
of John's witnessing. Even so the earlier Scriptures are superseded because they fulfilled their
purpose, not because they failed.

Some speak as though the progress of sacred narrative were like that of classic story—legend gently
shading into sober history. But this is false. The
miracles of Scripture are not found in the earlier
as distinct from the later books. They are found
at all the critical periods of the history, as when a
new dispensation is founded, or when the fate of
the covenant people is trembling in the balance.
The greatest is the last. All miracles, all prophecies, culminate in the life and work of Jesus
Christ. Not among the world's grey fathers,—
simple men no doubt,—but in a time of culture and

E

worn-out belief, was the God Incarnate seen, His life standing out as the most stupendous of miracles —a miracle even on the page of history.   There is a progress from legend to history between Hercules and Alexander of Macedon, between Numa Pompilius and Augustus Cæsar ; but it is not so between Abraham, God's friend, and Jesus Christ, God's own Son.

LECTURE III.

ALTHOUGH we have seen good reason to ascribe
to our Bible as a whole a claim to truth, unity,
and authority, a claim to be the Word of God,
we have not attempted to show how those books
were collected into one and regarded as one. To
begin this inquiry is the object of the present
lecture. We have to dwell for some time on points
of contact between the Old Testament and the
New, in order to bring out the position of the
New Testament.

At the very outset we are struck with the
remarkable phenomenon that we have before us.
This is not a book in any ordinary sense. The Old
Testament is a national literature. It was being
composed during 1500 years, and in very varied
circumstances. In the desert and in the city, in
anarchy and in tranquillity, the men of God wrote
by the Holy Ghost. Some parts of it are books
to be read, and some are to be sung ; some are
clearly didactic, others exuberantly poetical, touch-

ing every issue as well as every spring of national and personal life. But nevertheless, when it is gathered into one volume, its unity, as we have seen, is as striking as its variety.

So, too, is it with the New Testament to a great extent. Not as regards time. The New Testament claims to be written by the men of the generation that saw Jesus Christ in the flesh. In many other respects, however, it is as varied as the older volume by the side of which it has been set. Eight men—perhaps nine men—wrote it. Some parts of it were written in Europe, some in Asia, some in the wilds of Patmos. One book seems to have been written in congenial loneliness; several were dictated while the author's hand was chained to that of a Roman soldier. History, prophecy, and law are here as in the Hebrew Scripture; something corresponding to the Psalms is wanting to make the parallel complete. A change of form, too, to this extent, that while Old Testament prophets usually spoke before they wrote the revealing word, and then wrote what they had spoken, the New Testament prophets, even when they wrote to those whom they had taught by word of mouth, made their compositions take the form of letters, not of 'burdens' or addresses. Still the variety is wonderful, and the unity of the whole is amazing. That a pointed narrative like St. Mark's Gospel, and a meditative treatise like St. John's, written

with a different purpose, with nearly half a century
between them, and in different continents, should
tell of the same Divine Man ; and that the personality of this God-Man delineated by all the four
Gospels should be—unchanged yet glorified—the
centre of the Epistles of Paul and James and Jude
and Peter and John, is in itself supernatural. The
books which make up the New Testament are so
varied that to the mind of man there is perplexity
in the attempt to understand how they came to be
one, and to be recognised as one by the mass of the
people.   How came it about that Christians be-
thought themselves of the possibility of so blending
instruction with worship, that in their daily meetings the reading of the sacred books should form
a part of their service of God?   It does not appear
that in any previous religion men had attained
to the knowledge that not sacrifice but spiritual
service of God was the highest worship.   Christians
realized this, and also that the core of each service
lay in hearkening to the voice of the living God, at
first speaking through His divinely-commissioned
disciples, but soon—in their absence—through the
reading of the words which they had written.   We
search in vain for a parallel to this.   Though
hymns were used in the great services and in the
private devotions of the followers of many religions,
we do not find in the shrines of Egypt or Assyria,
any more than in those of India or China or Peru,

that the sacred books were regarded as the centre of the religion and of the worship.[1]

Not at any time before the Christian era was there a parallel to this even in Jerusalem. During the glory of the first temple the tables of the covenant were indeed by the side of the ark; yet it was not to those ancient writings, but to the presence of God on the mercy-seat, the covering of the ark, that men's hearts turned when they thought of the most solemn rites of their faith. While the second temple stood, and even when Herod's gorgeous pile crowned the height of Moriah, it was under the influence of a pathetic reminiscence of the departed glory that men still regarded the sacrificial ritual in that great house as the most acceptable worship of the God of their fathers. When Josephus speaks of his countrymen as ready to die for the books they so dearly loved, we have a testimony from about the time when the last survivor of the disciples was writing his Gospel, a century after Christ was born. So long as the temple stood, the most sacred services of religion were identified with its public sacrifices, and not with reading and prayer.

---

[1] There is little information as yet available on the important subject of the relation of the standard or authoritative books (if there were any) to the popular faith and ordinary ritual. The case of Egypt is an illustration of our ignorance. Again, we know very little of the means whereby (books not existing) the people of Greece or Rome were taught the theology of their religious services. The students of comparative religion have a large field in this department uncultivated. We know about the Brahmanical use of standard books, and that is almost all.

It was out of the synagogue that habitual reading, like so much else of the early Christian worship, grew. Perhaps we should add that the sacred supremacy of the word thus read was not fully realized in the synagogue until after Christianity had influenced it. In the synagogue before the time of Christ the traditions of the elders outweighed the voice of God in the written word. But still it was in the synagogue that the practice of reverently reading the Scripture as an integral part of divine worship took its rise. A more powerful source of influence and custom there could not be. Let us see how the synagogue led the Jews to be so much devoted to the written word. At the time of our Lord there were synagogues in every village,—about five hundred of them in Jerusalem alone,—and in them all there was the sacred roll of Scripture, which was habitually read when the congregation assembled. It might be read in the original Hebrew or in the Greek version (certainly the latter in Egypt), but it was expounded in the local vernacular. The three divisions of the Jewish Bible were not on the same level as regards this public reading. The *first* division — 'the law,' or, as we should say, the Pentateuch — had been from an early date read every Sabbath, being so subdivided into 153 portions that the whole of it was read through every three years : 'Moses of old time hath in

every city them that preach him, being read in the
synagogue every Sabbath-day' (Acts xv. 21).   The
second division—'the prophets,' including not only
what we call the prophets (Daniel excepted), but
also the historical books from Joshua to Kings—
was also regularly read.   This was not so old a
custom as that of reading the law.   It was said to
have begun when Antiochus Epiphanes (B.C. 168)
made it a capital crime for any one to have in his
possession the book of the covenant.   So eager were
the Jews to hear the sacred word that, when they
were forbidden to read the books of Moses, they
began the public reading of the prophets.[1]   In the
more peaceful times of which our New Testament
tells, both the law and the prophets were regularly
read: 'After the reading of the law and the prophets'
(Acts xiii. 15, see Acts xv. 21, 2 Cor. iii. 14), and the
phrase 'the law and the prophets' meant the well-
known Bible (Matt. xi. 13, xxii. 40).   The prophetical
books seem to have been read at the close of the
service, the name of the sections into which they
were subdivided—Haphtaroth (פָּטַר, to cleave, to let
go)—meaning dismissal.[2]   Thus it was that in the
synagogue of Nazareth the service was at an end
with the reading from Isaiah (probably the section

---

[1] See Wetstein on St. Luke iv. 17.   It is said that the reader must not
read less than twenty-one verses from the prophets, unless there were
a sermon, in which case about a third sufficed for reading.

[2] This suggests the similar phrase, 'missa est'—it is done—for the
close of the Christian worship, whence most probably the word 'mass.'
Others derive 'mass' from *mensa*.

for the day, as in Acts viii. 32), when the towns-
men of Jesus rose in wrath to cast Him out of the
city and over the rocks (Luke iv. 17, 30). The
third division—the 'Kethubim,' or writings—was
not, as a whole, regularly read through, though
portions [1] were fixed for prescribed feast days. The
Psalms, the first book in this division,[2] were regularly used liturgically in the synagogue as they
had been used in the temple. They were divided
into five books, to make them correspond with the
five books of Moses. Thus, though the other books
were occasionally read, the books in fixed and constant use were ' the law, and the prophets, and the
Psalms,' and to them Jesus appealed for their testimony concerning Himself (Luke xxiv. 44).[3]

In this way every Jew was accustomed to the
idea of sacred books being used in worship, and was
in the habit of appealing to them, and talking and
thinking of them as the rule of life and the standard
of doctrine. The passages or portions had their
descriptive names, which were as familiar to the
Jewish ear as favourite portions like the 23d Psalm
and the 14th of John are to Christian people. 'Have

---

[1] These portions were of the Megilloth, *i.e.* Song of Solomon, Ruth,
Lamentations, Ecclesiastes, Esther. '

[2] In the oldest Talmudic tradition Ruth came first, then Psalms.

[3] The present arrangement for the synagogue is Psalms, Proverbs,
Job = Kethubim Rischonim (first or early Kethubim); Canticles, Ruth,
Lamentations, Ecclesiastes, Esther = Kethubim Ketanim (or little
Kethubim); Daniel, Ezra, Nehemiah, Chronicles = Kethubim Acheronim
(or late Kethubim). The date of the arrangement is uncertain.

ye not read in the book of Moses, in the section called
The Bush?' (Mark xii. 26) ; 'Wot ye not what the
Scripture saith in the section about Elijah?' (Rom.
xi. 2).   This custom of naming the sections after
their principal subject re-appears in the manuscripts
of the New Testament, and lists of them were often
given at the beginning of a MS.   Thus, 'About
the magi,' 'About the children that were killed,'
begin the list of subjects in MSS. of St. Matthew.
Whatever may have been the case at an earlier
period, it was to the written word, and not to the
living voice of any one inspired of God to be a
preacher, that, when our Lord appeared, the Jew
had recourse in his deepest moods of earnestness :
'Ye search the Scriptures, because ye think that in
them ye have eternal life' (John v. 39).   The men in
the synagogue of Berea 'examined the Scriptures
daily whether these things were so' (Acts xvii. 11).
And when the first Christian teachers proclaimed
the gospel, they constantly repeated their Master's
first sermon by quoting the Old Testament, and
proving that the Scripture had been fulfilled in their
ears (Luke iv. 21).   The deference of all men to the
written word had been carried so far that men were
slaves of the mere letter, so that absurdly minute
subjects of controversy were discussed, the number
of letters in the Bible was counted, the commandments were apportioned as greater and less, and so
on, until the very masters of Israel had no concep-

tion of the Spirit which truly filled the word. No
man was 'speaking with authority,' because men had
lost their practical faith in the living God who
spoke in time past to the fathers.

But still this fact meets us, that the mind of the
Jew was familiar with the idea of Holy Scripture.
Nor only this, but with the idea of a Canon that
was closed. The word 'canon' was not known for
400 years in this distinct sense of a standard collection of books, but all that we mean by it was
familiar. It had not entered into the mind of a
Jew for ages that some new book might perhaps
be made and added to the Canon of his Divine
Scripture. The book had been sealed for generations, and no hope had for long entered the pious
mind that the dumb oracles of God would speak
again until Messiah came. Judas Maccabæus pulled
down the altar of burnt-offerings which was pro-
faned, and laid up the stones in a convenient place
until there should come a prophet to show what
should be done with them (1 Macc. iv. 46 ; see also
ix. 27, xiv. 41). 'I know that Messias cometh,
which is called Christ : when He is come, He will
declare unto us all things,' said the woman of
Samaria (John iv. 25).

This conclusion seems to rest on ascertained
facts. There is nothing in the threefold division
or in the nature and amount of acceptance of the
Hebrew Canon to make it doubtful. There has

been at times great faith placed in the recent Jewish tradition that Ezra founded a Great Synagogue of learned men which compiled the Canon and fixed it. This rests on no good authority; but it is only a popular and legendary way of accounting for the fact that an authoritative Canon existed.[1] While many theories have been published among us regarding the age of some of the books of the Old Testament, there can scarcely be doubt or denial that the Hebrew Canon which we now have was the Jewish Bible in the days of Christ. Even if there were some doubts of Esther at that time, or in the early Christian centuries, they were no more than exist on the same subject in our own day. The book of Esther was written to record a marvellous deliverance of the Jews in the Persian Empire, and to commend the observance of the feast of Purim in memory of it. The festival came from a foreign land, and although eventually it became most popular, it does not seem to have occupied any such place when Christ was upon earth; and indeed its chief popularity was of later date, when the Jews, who interpolated curses in the reading of the villainies of Haman, could think of the Christians and mentally curse them when they anathematized the memory of their Persian foe. The slow acceptance of the

[1] The men of the Great Synagogue are said to have written Ezekiel, the Twelve Prophets, Daniel, and Esther. Some think that this refers to the Assembly convened by Nehemiah.

book was due to its being without any mention
of the Divine Being, and to its having a foreign
origin.

So also it is quite true that Daniel's place was
not among the prophets as in our Bible, but
among the miscellaneous writings which formed
the third division of the Canon.   But this does
not mean that Daniel was of small account in
those days.   The Alexandrian translators, followed
by the Vulgate and other versions, set Daniel after
Ezekiel as the fourth of the major prophets.
Though the date of this is uncertain, it cannot
have been very late.   But the Hebrew Canon set
him among the miscellaneous writings.   It is not
easy to say why.   The idea of some Jewish commentators, that the three divisions marked the
three degrees of inspiration, the law, the prophets, and the 'writings' representing a descend-
ing scale, is sufficiently disproved by the fact that
in the third division were the Psalms.   It seems
most probable that chronology decided the place
of the divisions of the Jewish Bible, though not
of the books within each division.   The law came
before the prophets ; but the prophets, which
included the history, came before the miscellaneous
writings.   And hence the order of those three
divisions.   But the second and third divisions were
not regarded as closed till long after the first of
the books in them were accepted as divine ; and

dates do not seem to have decided the place of
the several books. Thus in the second division,
Jeremiah, though a later prophet, was before
Hosea and Amos. In the third division, Ruth
comes after the Psalms, which was long an unfinished book ; Ezra, Nehemiah, after Esther.
And in the third division also, Canticles and
Ecclesiastes, which were believed to be Solomon's,
were set beside Esther.[1] These books, with Ruth
and Lamentations, were called *Megilloth* or volumes,
because they were each written on a separate roll.
The position of Daniel in the Hebrew Bible,
therefore, before Ezra and Nehemiah, in the same
subdivision with them[2] and Chronicles, does not
give us much assurance as to his age, although it
increases our perplexity when we find him so far
from Ezekiel, and not beside the other prophets
of the captivity or of the return.

It is more important, and it is for our present
purpose sufficient, to keep in mind that whatever
may have been the principle on which particular
books were assigned to their several places in the
Hebrew Canon, or the principle on which the
order was so varied, that Canon itself was regarded

---

[1] Even if we accept the Jewish subdivision into Kethubim Rishonim,
Ketanim, and Acheronim (see before, p. 73, note), we cannot see how in
this last class should be included Daniel, Ezra, Nehemiah, and Chronicles,
while Esther is in the previous class along with the works of Solomon.

[2] It does not seem possible to hold by 'subjectivity' as the character-
istic of the third division. This might perhaps give a place to Daniel,
but not to Ezra, Nehemiah, and Esther.

as closed before our Lord came, in this sense that
no one thought of adding to it. It is absurd to
magnify the controversies regarding this or that
book into a general uncertainty as to there being
a Canon. The LXX. was made two or three centuries before Christ; the Hebrew Canon was complete before that time ; and the lingering disputes
no more unsettled the whole question of a Canon
than disputes in our own day as to Jude or Peter
unsettle it. Doubts as to Esther came down into
the Christian Church, though the Jews exalted its
popularity, and these doubts have an existence (only
half-acknowledged) in our own day. The doubts as
to Solomon's Song are said to have been ended by
the strong assertion of Rabbi Akiba (about A.D.
120), that the day it was made was the best day
the world ever saw.[1] There were doubts as to
Ecclesiastes also. But those difficulties regarded
the right of four or five particular books to be in
the Canon ; the very doubts show that the fact of
a Canon existing was well understood. No one
supposed that any new book could be added to it,
or that any book was in it which was of later date
than about a century after the Babylonian exile.
The dispute as to the writings of Solomon had
reference only to their being really Solomon's.
Had they been known to be of later date they

---

[1] 'No day in the whole history of the world is of so much worth as
the one in which the Song of Songs was given to Israel; for all the
Scriptures are holy, but the Song of Songs is most holy.'

would not have been considered at all. The book
of Daniel, too, would not have been in the Canon
had not the Jews believed that it was the work
of the worthy whose name was so great among the
men of the captivity that Ezekiel reckoned him
with Noah and Job (Ezek. xiv. 14, 20, xxviii. 3).
Josephus was expressing the Jewish conviction
when he said :

> 'We have not myriads of books incongruous and conflicting ;
> there are among us only two-and-twenty books which have the
> record of all time, which are justly accepted as divine. . . . From
> the death of Moses till the reign of Artaxerxes, who succeeded
> Xerxes as king of the Persians, the prophets following Moses
> wrote the things done in their times in thirteen books.   The
> remaining four contain hymns to God, and counsels for men.
> But from the time of Artaxerxes until our times, there have
> indeed been several books written, but they have not been
> accounted worthy of like credit to those which were earlier,
> because there was not the exact succession of prophets since that
> time.[1] And how firmly we have given credit to those books of
> our own nation is evident by what we do ; for during so many
> ages as have already passed, no one has been so bold as either
> to add anything to them, or to take anything from them, or to
> make any change in them ; but it is become natural to all Jews,
> immediately and from their very birth, to esteem those books to
> contain divine doctrines, and to persist in them, and if occasion be,
> willingly to die for them ' (C. Apion, i. 8).

We have been speaking of the Hebrew Canon
because it was the original and the true Canon.

---

[1] Josephus' enumeration of 22 is thus made up : *Five* books of Moses.
Thirteen prophets, viz.—1. Joshua ; 2. Judges and Ruth ; 3. Samuel ;
4. Kings ; 5. Chronicles ; 6. Ezra and Nehemiah ; 7. Esther ; 8. Isaiah ;
9. Jeremiah and Lamentations ; 10. Ezekiel ; 11. Daniel ; 12. the
Twelve Minor Prophets ; 13. Job (?). *Four* books of hymns and counsels,
viz. Psalms and the writings of Solomon.

The Alexandrian Canon, which we find in the Septuagint Version, was not so soon closed. The origin of this Version is obscure, but we may assume that it (or at least the Pentateuch part of it) was made in Egypt during the reign of Ptolemy Soter, or of his son Philadelphus, B.C. 298–247, who wished to complete the great library by adding to it the sacred books of the Jews. The idea therefore does not seem to have sprung from Jewish piety, but from the literary taste of an enlightened heathen. Not only did Ptolemy set the Jewish Bible in his library, but he signalized the event by ransoming at great cost the Jewish captives in his kingdom, more than 100,000 in number. The Pentateuch was not only the first, but also the most carefully translated portion of the Old Testament, and the other books were translated not very long afterwards, though there seems to have been no authoritative revision or even unity of work. Among commercial Jews in cities on the Mediterranean, and in Palestine itself, Greek became more and more the language of daily use; and a Greek translation of the Scriptures was indispensable if the Bible was to be intelligently used in the synagogue. Even when the Bible was read in Hebrew, there was given a translation or paraphrase in Aramaic or Greek, as the case might be. But the fixed translation soon superseded paraphrases, and before the

Christian era the Septuagint had in many places supplanted the Hebrew in the estimation of ordinary Jews. After Christianity prevailed, the Greek grew in popular favour with Christians; many of the Fathers, from Irenæus onwards (some of them ignorant of Hebrew), ascribed inspiration to the translation as well as to the original. The fabulous story as to the translators being shut up in separate cells, and upon conference finding that they had miraculously hit upon the same words in their translation, a story which with many variations is found in many places, shows how great was the reverence paid to the Greek. We find the first form of the legend in a statement that the translators were prophets, agreeing by inspiration on the terms they used. In this belief Jews and others went to the Isle of Pharos to hold a yearly festival in honour of the great work of translation which was there accomplished. But at a later date we read (Justin) of the translators being in seventy cells, or by twos in thirty-six cells; always with the same miraculous agreement in the end when they compared their notes.[1] In this Greek Old Testament there are additions made to the Hebrew Daniel, and Esther, and Chronicles, and Jeremiah; and whole books (as 2 Esdras, 2 Macc., and Wisdom) are added, of which no part ever existed in Hebrew.

[1] Josephus is too cautious to say all this, *Ant.* xii. 2.

There is nothing surprising in this. The natural result of large commercial intercourse with many lands is to make men tolerant, considerate, and eclectic. It also tends to a loose grasp of first principles in matters where personal interests are not immediately concerned. And thus the Alexandrian who was in the emporium of the world saw much that was good in many systems and religions which acknowledged no good in one another. He anticipated to a large extent the modern study of comparative religion; the sympathetic study, that is to say, with the purpose and hope of discovering what is best in each and what is common to all. Even a Hebrew felt the influence of the place; and while he preferred his nation and its books to everything else in the world, he did not feel so assured as were his kindred still in Palestine that the age of prophecy and of revelation had come to a close. The Jew of Palestine believed that no books in the whole world were to be put near to those which Jehovah had given to the Hebrew fathers; the tongue of Abraham and of Jacob was the one only language of inspiration. All books of Greek origin were worthless to him in comparison with the Hebrew books; and he would have none of them. But the Jew of Alexandria, just because those Greek books spake to him in the language of his daily life, was inclined to welcome them. He read

Moses in the Greek tongue; he had felt the
potency of inspired teaching through the medium
of that translation. So when another Greek book
came to him, claiming to have been written in
Hebrew, and almost asserting that it was inspired,
he was not inclined to reject it. Its words were:
'I will yet pour forth doctrine as prophecy,
and leave it to all ages for ever. Behold that
I have not laboured for myself only, but for all
them that seek wisdom' (Ecclus. xxiv. 33, 34).
It seemed to him that the Spirit of wisdom,
of which that same book sang as not only
'established in Zion,' but as 'taking root in
an honourable people, even in the portion of
the Lord's inheritance' (Ecclus. xxiv. 10, 12),
might still be surviving and speaking unto
men.[1] That book, indeed, was said to have been
originally in Hebrew. But another notable book
which was never written in Hebrew said:
'Wisdom in all ages, entering into holy souls,
maketh friends of God and prophets' (Wisd.
vii. 27). In the spirit of that claim the Alexandrian Jew gave sacred reverence to many
books from which his Palestinian brother turned
away with scorn. Into his translation of the most
sacred Hebrew books also crept certain additions,
as when translations of Baruch[2] and of the

---

[1] See Oehler, Art. 'Kanon' in Herzog's *Realencyc.* vii. 255.

[2] Said by Origen to have been in some Hebrew texts of the Old
Testament.

Epistle of Jeremiah were added to the writings of Jeremiah in the Septuagint Version of the Bible.

Thus it came about that in the LXX. or Bible of the Hellenistic—or foreign—Jews were many books or portions of books not in the Hebrew Canon. Those are the writings known to us as The Apocrypha. It also followed that among the Hellenists the Canon could not be regarded as closed at the same time and in the same sense as among the Hebrew-speaking Jews.

But, nevertheless, it is not correct to speak as though even the Hellenists regarded the Canon as open, or attached to those added books the same authority as to the Bible itself. Philo is the best representative of the Hellenist, and he never quotes an Apocryphal book, although his notions of inspiration were so elastic that he claimed to be himself inspired. His mode of handling the law of Moses shows that he recognised revelation as a special form of inspiration.[1] The Fourth Book of Esdras speaks of only twenty-four books openly published so that all men may read, thus ignoring the Apocryphal additions. We have seen that Josephus, who, however, to a certain extent admits the additions to Esther, distinguishes between the canonical books and all those of later date. He was not, like Philo, an Alexandrian sage ; but he

[1] Philo, *De Vita Contempl.* § 3.

thoroughly understood the position of his countrymen in all lands.

On the whole, therefore, we must conclude that,
while the Alexandrian Bible in common use contained many additions to the Hebrew Bible, and
while doubtless the ordinary readers were likely
to set the original and the additions on the same
level, there is no good ground for concluding that
the more thoughtful Jews, even of Alexandria, had
lost the principle of the distinction between what
we may call canonical and extra-canonical books.
In the Christian Church, under the influence of
the same conditions, the fathers—after Justin
Martyr, who never directly cites the Apocrypha—
were chargeable with a far higher exaltation of
the Greek Apocrypha than the Jews themselves
were.   It was on account of Christian preferences
that such men as Origen did not venture to
remove from the Old Testament what was not
found in the original Hebrew text.   He says of
the additions to Esther, that it would be ill-done
to reject the sacred books in their form received by
Christians, and to defer to the Jews; and that
such rejection would also throw doubt on the
loving care of Divine Providence for the word
which He had given to those for whom Christ
died (*Letter to Africanus*, p. 14).   The Christian
predilection for the Greek Version, as being understood at first over nearly the whole known world;

the fact that the old Latin Version was translated
from it and not from the Hebrew, and contained
all its books ; and the favour of leading Christians
for individual books contained in the Apocryphal
portions,—tended to drive all non-Christian Jews
everywhere (and the Nazarene Christians also) into
a more devoted adherence to the Hebrew Canon ;
and as Hebrew learning revived, as rabbinical
teachings were preserved and classified, the Hebrew
Bible and the Hebrew Canon rose to entire pre-
dominance among the Jews, while some Christians
were superstitiously ascribing inspiration to the
Greek translators from whom came the Septuagint.[1]
At a later time the Jews held a yearly fast on
account of the translation. Darkness covered the
earth for three days, they said, when the law was
written in Greek in the days of King Ptolemy.
Even among the Christians the deliberate changes
in the Hebrew Canon are confined to the omission
of Esther and the addition of Baruch ;[2] and the
Hebrew Canon as a whole is the only one distinctly recognised during the first four centuries,
though individual Christian writers (as Clement
of Alexandria) reverenced single books in the
Greek supplementary collection.

---

[1] Irenæus, iii. 25; Clem. Alex., *Strom.* i. 22, § 149 ; Aug., *Civ. Dei*,
xviii. 43. See Justin Martyr, *Dial.* chap. 68, in proof of *his* saying
one thing and Jews another about the LXX.

[2] See the catalogues in Westcott's article 'Canon' in Smith's
Dictionary of the Bible, vol. i. p. 256.

And what, then, was the view of the first Christians? What was the position taken by Jesus Himself? It is remarkable, but after the facts we have noted it is not surprising, that Jesus Christ never quotes the Apocrypha. Nor does any one of His apostles whose writings have come down to us. There are passages in the Epistles which refer to Jewish legends or traditions, as when Jude speaks of Michael's contention with Satan for the body of Moses, or when the writer to the Hebrews recounts some incidents of Maccabean martyrdom; but those allusions to a knowledge of history or tradition outside of the Bible are very different from the use of the Old Testament. Not incidentally, but habitually, the writers of the New .Testament lean upon the Old Testament for proof of doctrine, even for the test of truth. And of any such use of any book outside of the Hebrew Canon there is not a trace. There are some real and some apparent quotations from other sources, but at the most they are only literary quotations. It may be a mere coincidence, but it is at least noteworthy, that the only books of the Old Testament not quoted in the New are the three books of the writings of Solomon, Esther, and Ezra and Nehemiah. Ezra and Nehemiah are historical books, which there was probably no occasion to quote; but the other four unquoted books—Esther, Proverbs, Ecclesiastes, and Can-

ticles—are those books which were not accepted
by all at the time of our Lord. Our Lord's example of reverence for the Old Testament was
followed by the disciples, who habitually read it
in their meetings, as had been customary in the
synagogue. The reading of the Old Testament
was thus an integral part of Christian worship from
the first, as we may learn explicitly from a well-
known passage in Justin Martyr's *First Apology*.
' On the day called Sunday all dwellers in town or
country are convened, and the memoirs of the
apostles and the writings of the prophets are read
so long as time permits' (Justin, *Apol.* i. c. 67).
And again the same writer says : ' When ye hear
the prophets read as though they were personally
addressing you, do not count that what is said
comes from men self-inspired, but regard it as
coming from the Divine Logos that moved them'
(c. 36). Ignatius speaks of the prophets whose
announcements led up to the gospel. And so
with the other fathers. They all teach, as Paul
taught, that the Old Testament is Scripture inspired of God, and therefore profitable for doctrine,
for reproof, for correction, and for instruction in
righteousness (2 Tim. iii. 16). They had learned
from Christ Himself to teach the Jews. ' If ye
believed Moses, ye would believe me : for he wrote
of me' (John v. 46).

Thus, then, we find that, when our Lord came to

the earth, there was a collection of sacred writings believed to be closed—a collection to which no word had been added for several hundred years. Jesus Himself acknowledged the authority of this sacred book, and at the outset of His ministry declared that He did not come to destroy but to fulfil it (Matt. v. 17). His apostles never failed to make solemn and special acknowledgment of the divine authority of that book, all whose words must needs be fulfilled. In their estimation, no word had been spoken like it ; the other things which men prided themselves upon and studied were cunningly devised fables or mere traditions of men. 'But the things which God foreshadowed by the mouth of all the prophets, that Christ should suffer, He thus ful- filled' (Acts iii. 18). 'Yea, and all the prophets from Samuel and them that followed after, as many as have spoken, they also told of these days' (Acts iii. 24).

The marvellous claim of the writers of the New Testament acquires its chief significance when we keep in mind this conviction of theirs, and of all men's, regarding the Old Testament. They claim for their own writings a place beside those sacred books. It is not possible to deny that every one of them, from the beginning of the New Testament to the end of it, asserts that he writes by the inspiration of the living God, whose word is the Old Testament Scripture. The Evangelists do not, indeed, obtrude their own personality, but they claim to write as men that had reaped the fruits of the Spirit promised as the Paraclete, who was sent to teach the truth and the meaning of the life of Christ. They not only record certain words as having come from the lips of the Master, but they often undertake explicitly to say what those words meant [e.g. 'He spake of the temple of His body'], and they always imply that the meaning was that which they convey. When Jesus had risen from the dead, they say that they understood the meaning of the words He had used. The question on which evidence is being taken in the ceaseless controversy of the Church with the world, is that of their being truthful men; but we must not therefore forget that, if this be granted, then it follows that they were men guided by God in what they had to say. There is not in any other book which has come down to us a claim like that made by those historians, who assert with undemonstrative confidence that they are trustworthy interpreters of the mystery of godliness which was manifest in the flesh when Jesus Christ dwelt among men. A book which made such a claim as this, and which made it good, must of necessity take the first place in human reverence and esteem.

Take, in the same way, the Epistles. Take the earliest of them, the Thessalonian letters of St. Paul (1 Thess. ii. 13). There is, on his part, no

hesitation in making a claim of authority when he
says that the word the Thessalonians had heard
was not the word of men, but of a verity the word
of God, or when he reminds them, in the Second
Epistle, that his is a saving word, in which they
are bound to stand fast and firm. 'So then,
brethren, stand fast, and hold the traditions which
ye were taught, whether by word, or by epistle of
ours' (2 Thess. ii. 15). He tells the Corinthians
(1 Cor. vii. 17) that he gives authoritative direction
(διατάσσομαι) in all the churches of the Lord. He
dares to say an anathema to fermenting Galatia on
the man or the angel who teaches a different gospel
from his—from his which he received neither from
a human source nor by human means, but through
the direct and immediate agency of Jesus Christ
and of God the Father.

John's First Epistle begins with the declaration
that, when the writer speaks of the manifestation
of life in the Word, he tells of that which he
thoroughly knew on the evidence of his mind and
his senses, but he significantly appends to that
statement the assurance that his 'fellowship' was
with the Father and the Son Jesus Christ, and that
his object in writing was that his readers might
be raised to the same fellowship. Throughout the
Epistle he writes from within the sanctuary of
fellowship with God, without doubt or misgiving
as to his authority. The seer of the Apocalypse

denounces woes upon all who tamper with the words of his prophecy, and calls on all men to hear what the Spirit said through him to the churches.

There is no such explicit claim in the Epistle of James; but James uses the words and the authority of the Old Testament prophets in such a way as to challenge comparison of the substance and the form of his message with theirs. No book of the New Testament takes this position more distinctly; and when we keep in mind that James wrote to the twelve tribes, to the men who, unlike the heathen, had a Bible and obeyed it, and looked up to it as the voice of God, the deliberate claim made by this Christian teacher to occupy the same position as the prophets of ancient Israel is specially significant.

Peter, though humble and penitent, always writing like a man under the shadow of the great denial, still took the position of one who had a commission to teach, who looked back to the sufferings of Christ as a witness, and forward to the glory in which he would share; one who had received a special charge to feed the flock of God, and who could therefore without presumption exhort even the elders (1 Peter v. 1), and could declare that the living voice of God from on high had made the old word of prophecy more sure.

And even Jude not only claims a right to exhort, but calls upon his beloved readers to remember the words which had been spoken before by the apostles

of our Lord Jesus Christ.   The meaning of this is
clearly, as in Second Peter, to build up the Church
in that faith which was expounded in the words not
only of Christian teachers but of Christian writers
(2 Peter iii. 16).   When Peter refers to the Epistles
of his beloved brother Paul as 'Scriptures' which
'the ignorant and unstedfast wrest, as they do also
the other Scriptures, unto their own destruction,'
he is claiming for Paul's writings a place beside
the ancient Bible of the Jews.

And this, as we have shown in detail, is the
remarkable and indeed unparalleled claim made by
the New Testament as a whole, and admitted by
the Christian Church with full knowledge of its
significance.[1]

---

[1] The foregoing argument and statement are of course directly contra-
dictory of the theory that the early Christians did not admit the special
inspiration or divine authority of any other books than those of the
O. T., which had come down to them from remote antiquity.   'The Holy
Ghost,' says Reuss (*Gesch. der heiligen Schriften Gesch. N. T.*, § 285),
'who once rested on a few prophets only, had now been shared in by
all the chosen of Christ, and nobody was able and willing to ascribe to
himself or to any other disciple an exclusive inspiration.'   And in his
notes he observes that in the enumeration of gifts (Rom. xii. and
1 Cor. xii.) there is no special gift of writing.   But it must, on the
other hand, be observed that St. Paul and the other writers of the
N. T. claimed for themselves this very thing, that they had *authority
to write*.   They stood apart from the rest, first of all as apostles,
whose calling in the Church was of God (and 'not of men, neither by
men, nor through men,' as others were called); and when Paul wrote,
he explicitly asserted that his were regulative and decisive words in
writing as they were when spoken.   Theories that when 'the Holy
Ghost fell on all,' then all were raised to the level of the apostles, must
be recast, if it is intended to make them consistent with the facts.

LECTURE IV.

WHEN we seek to look more closely into the
history of the reception of our Christian books in
the Church, we are met by the fact of a great
chasm in our annals. The early years of Christian
history have no record save what we find in the
New Testament itself. Even that is fragmentary.
The life of the Lord is told with some fulness by
the four Evangelists, but regarding the next
period—the first period of the Church when the
Lord had risen—we have only a few detached
notices in one book, the Acts of the Apostles,
and we glean some things from allusions in the
Epistles, which bring us down to about the middle
of the first century. The second half of that
century is nearly blank. From the time when we
leave Paul in his own hired house at Rome, a
hundred years come and go before we have any
connected narrative of the fortunes of the Church of
Christ. At the end of that time we are on the
beaten paths of history ; but during its course the

whole fortunes of the Church had changed.   The
little seed had become a tree.   The apostles had
gone to and fro over the Roman world, from India to
Spain; persecutors had thought to scatter congregations, but had only multiplied the preachers of the
Word ; and the Church of the Crucified Jesus was a
powerful force in the world, drawing the attention of
emperors and their subordinates,[1] to remove whose
misconceptions of its purposes and functions the
most eloquent writers of the Church employed all
their force and skill.   The result was, as we have
already learned from Justin Martyr about A.D. 140,
that congregations were organized everywhere, and
in their ordinary meetings were engaged in reading
the memoirs of the apostles along with the prophetic writings of the Old Testament.   It would
appear that the claim advanced by the books of the
New Testament had been admitted by the Church.
Our present purpose is to try to indicate how that
admission was made, how it grew from less to more
distinct, until before the end of the second century
the New Testament was the book as we now have
it.   The second century is the battle-ground of
criticism.   With the testimony of Irenæus towards
the end of it, and of Clement of Alexandria and
Tertullian at its close, we attain to ground which is
no longer debateable.   Indeed I believe it may

---

[1] See Pliny's *Letter to Trajan*, and the 'Imperial Edicts,' *Canonicity*,
pp. 362–367.

now be said that the debate does not extend
beyond the middle of the century, so that we can
prove the books of our New Testament to have
been in the hands of men who had met and talked
with the apostles of the Lord.   I believe it can
be proved that the Church was built upon the
revelation of God which we have in the New
Testament; and that from the very first it recognised in those books the truth out of which, as
proclaimed by apostles and disciples, it had taken
its rise.   These are, if we may so say, the pro-
positions to be maintained in this lecture.

Let us understand what is the argument on the
other side.   It is that Christianity as now ex-
hibited in the New Testament is not the original
Christianity of Christ, but a development, sometimes a perversion; that it is far more doctrinal, and
ascribes far higher attributes to the person of Christ
than either Jesus Himself or His first disciples
dreamed of.   We are told, that under the influence
of Paul, the Christian religion passed out of the
stage of ethical teaching into that of a doctrinal
edifice built upon Christ's own personality.   The
Gospels are therefore a legendary form of history,
the Christ of whom they tell is a growth very different from the Man of Nazareth, if His simple
life were truly told.   Many of the Epistles are, in
like manner, the outcome of the growth of the
Church, and are of later date.   Only Romans,

Corinthians (First and Second), and Galatians are genuine. The only other genuine book is the Apocalypse. It was Ferdinand Christian Baur, a Professor in Tübingen, who advocated those views so ably as to give his name to the school of critics now so well known. The point at issue is briefly this : Was the Church founded upon the truth contained in the New Testament, or was the New Testament founded on the ideas and aspirations of the Church ? In other words, did the Jesus Christ of the Gospels live and die as the Gospels tell, or do these Gospels represent the Church's view of what ought to have been ?

It is obvious that the counter argument suggested by this question has many subdivisions. There is an argument on grounds of reason to the effect that, without Jesus Christ as its founder,—the same Jesus Christ of whom the Church in the second century testified,—Christianity could never have had a beginning. There is an argument on the ground of general church history, which would show that the whole character of the Church is inconsistent with the occurrence of any important change at any date between its beginning and the middle of the second century. But the central argument comes under the head of Biblical Criticism, and its purport is that the scattered notices and allusions to the Redeemer's life and teaching, which we find in the surviving fragments of the first Christian literature, are consistent with the position of those who maintain that the New Testament faithfully and fully represents the facts upon which the first foundations of the Church were laid. In other words, we believe the answer of sound criticism to be, that the earliest literature shows that the Church possessed our Gospels and the mass of the other books of the New Testament during the first century. It is with this last form or sub-division of the answer to Baur that we are now to be engaged. What we have to state must be an outline, and no more, but we shall try to mark the chief points from one to the other of which a student must pass in filling up the outline. It is impossible for us in these lectures to enter into minute details concerning every book of the New Testament, or even regarding each of the books whose canonicity has been most disputed ; and I ask leave to refer my hearers who may be disposed to investigate the more particular grounds on which the general argument rests, to the detailed evidence which I have compiled elsewhere upon the subject of the Canon as a whole, and of each book in it.

We begin by repeating the conclusion to which we were brought at the close of last lecture. Before Jewish Christians—or any Christians who reverenced the revelation given through Moses—could think for a moment of setting any new books

alongside of the Old Testament, they must have
found new books which claimed, and claimed wor-
thily, to occupy that high ground. We found that
the books of the New Testament do make such a
claim, so that the place of canonicity to which they
attained is not one to which they 'came by acci-
dent.' It is an inheritance which they conquered
in accordance with their claim. For the present
form of our argument it is immaterial whether
they are all justified in making that claim. It
is not essential to our present purpose that the
Epistles ascribed to Jude and to Second Peter
be written by the disciples whose names they
bear, because our argument has been that all the
books which we find in the Canon claim a place
of authority for themselves—some claiming it for
themselves alone, and others not for themselves
alone, but for the whole of which they form a
part.

It is another step in the argument to maintain,
as we seek now to do, that from the earliest times
of which we have record those books were acknowledged to have made good their claim. In the early
days, when the Church was full of the new life
drawn from the Christ who had risen, her members
recognised those books as also full of it. The new
wine of the kingdom was found in those vessels,
the same, the very same, as the Church had drunk
when poured into her by the living hand of the

apostles and prophets and pastors of the first years. It is no light thing this. We have not merely intellectual assent to the claim of the books, but we have the testimony of all those churches that their amazing growth was due to their life being fed by the words which proceeded out of the mouth of God, and were contained in those precious Epistles and Gospels.

But it has often been alleged that the books which we now have were 'selected by the Church' from among a host of competitors, so that our Canon is really the result of a 'struggle for existence' in which the strongest won. There is a sense in which we not only admit this, but hold by it. Those books *were* the strongest, and at one time— the first time of their history—there were others in circulation which have perished from their side. But that there were other books making such a claim as theirs, and that those books have perished, is not only not an ascertained fact, but the ascertained facts are against it. And that the Church at any date, or at any succession of dates during the first two centuries, took counsel and resolved to put an end to the existence of some books, selecting certain others for honour and permanent estimation, is a grotesque impossibility. It is vain for an assailant to point to the opening words of Luke's Gospel, as though the third Evangelist entered into competition with many others. The position taken

by St. Luke is that many others had 'attempted'
something different from that orderly and con-
secutive narrative, beginning at the very beginning,
which it was in his power to write. That there
should be partial accounts or digests of the 'matters
fulfilled among us,' was to be expected,—the Church
in almost every locality must have had some such
fragmentary narratives and digests which 'many
took in hand to arrange,'—but St. Luke at once
stepped on another platform with his Gospel.

The nature of the case leads to our holding that
in this sense the strongest of many narratives are
the survivors ; but we have no proof of either gospel
or epistle like those now in our possession having
once existed and being subsequently lost. The
'Gospel of the Hebrews' is the only gospel which
can for a moment offer an apparent contradiction to
this statement. But it was not another and independent gospel, like the four now in our possession.
It was our Gospel of Matthew, with a few additions
made by the Jewish Christians among whom it
circulated. When those additions are collected,
and all the references to the book are compared
with each other, all that results is a Judæo-
Christian recension of the Gospel originally written
for the Hebrew disciples of Jesus.[1] Again, there
has been often said to be a lost Epistle of St. Paul
to the Laodiceans, although we have now little

---

[1] See *Canonicity*, p. 451.

doubt that our Epistle to the Ephesians was a
circular letter of which another copy was sent to
Laodicea.[1] Beyond those we have no sure ground
for believing that books which could have belonged
to our New Testament have been lost.

It is of no avail to say that there are still extant
books which were sometimes associated with our
New Testament in the public estimation of the
Church. There is not one such book which had
more than a local and temporary acceptance among
the books regularly used in worship. But, moreover, when such books were used, they could not be
competitors with our canonical books. All of them
which have come down to us from the early Church,
not only make no such claim, but they disclaim any
right to a place of authority, and testify to the pre-
eminence of the books of the New Testament.
Some critics have ignored this fact, and have argued
as though they had disposed of the books of the
New Testament when they have shown that other
books were read in the congregations of primitive
Christendom. Now it is quite true that Clement's
Epistle was publicly read, and 'Barnabas' and
'Hermas,' and that all of them are found in
manuscripts which contain the books of our New
Testament. Clement is found in the great Alexandrian MS. in the British Museum; Barnabas
(complete) and Hermas (partly) in the great

[1] See *Canonicity*, p. 237.

Sinaitic MS. But we do not admit that those facts prove the early copyists, and presumably the early Church, to have given them a place as high as that of our Canon. We do not deny that those books were so read; nay, we found on such reading. We admit that the books had liturgical authority; but we hold it to be impossible, when their own contents and claims are considered, that they could even have been set in a canonical position.

Take what is known as the Epistle of Clement. It is probably the earliest Christian writing outside of the New Testament, and is certainly a genuine product of the first century. When we look at it, we find first of all that it does not profess to come from any individual, but to be from the Church in Rome to the Church in Corinth. Early tradition connects it beyond all reasonable doubt with Clement as the first man in the Roman Church at the time, and consequently the writer of what bears the title of the Church. Still it is to be observed, that when authority is claimed for statements made, —when a distinct assurance of speaking the truth regarding doctrine or practice is found in it,—what might have been assumption on the part of an individual is justifiable in the case of a whole Church writing to counsel and warn another Church. The Corinthian Church had developed the spirit of faction against which St. Paul so earnestly wrote

in his First Epistle.   Its divisions had become a
scandal to all Christendom, and observant heathen
(chap. xlvii.) blasphemed the name of the Lord
when they saw the strifes and jealousies.   The
Roman Church therefore warn their brethren in
Corinth of the dangers of this evil state of things.
They speak as having, like them, received the
gospel from holy men who had since passed away.
For the authority on which they proceed they refer
to Paul's Epistles to those very Corinthians.   'Take
up the Epistle of the blessed Paul the apostle.
What was the first thing he wrote to you in the
beginning of the gospel ?   Truly he wrote to you
spiritually concerning himself and Cephas and
Apollos, because that even then partisanships had
been formed among you.   But that partisanship
of yours brought less sin upon you, because you
were partisans of apostles to whom all men have
witnessed, and of him (Apollos) whom they
honoured.   But now observe who they are that
have drawn you into factions (διέστρεψαν) and
have lessened the renown of your much-praised
brotherly love.   Disgraceful things, brethren, ay,
very disgraceful things, and unworthy of the
followers of Christ, are heard of you when it is
told us that the very strong·and ancient Church
of the Corinthians has been induced by two or
three persons to rebel against the presbyters.
And this report has not only come to us, but

also unto those who do not belong to us, so that blasphemies are brought upon the name of the Lord through your folly, and danger is incurred by yourselves.   Let us therefore remove this quickly out of the way, and let us fall down before the Master, and with tears entreat Him that in His mercy He become reconciled to us and restore us to the seemly and undefiled observance of brotherly love' (Clem., chaps. xlvii., xlviii.).

In another place the Roman Church rebuke the Corinthians for having removed from the eldership some elders who were doing their duties honourably and well; but the rebuke is based on the intention of the apostles that the men appointed to office should not lose it while they did well.   'Our apostles knew through the Lord Jesus Christ that there would be strife about the overseership' (chap. xliv.).   It is because of the authority of the apostles that the writers of the Roman letter are so sure of having truth and the mind of God upon their side. Notwithstanding one or two ambiguous passages, I do not think that it claims authority or power.[1]

---

[1] There is a request for prayer (chap. lvi.) that the offenders may yield not to the Romans but to the will of God.   And again, ' If there be some that disobey the things spoken by Him through us, let them know that they shall involve themselves in no small transgression and peril' (chap. lix.).   One more passage, which admits of another rendering, seems to be best translated thus: ' Ye shall provide for us joy and rejoicing if, becoming obedient to the things which we have written, ye, through the Holy Spirit, cut off the unhallowed wrath of your zeal according to the prayer which we have made for peace and like-mindedness in this epistle' (chap. lxiii.).   This meaning harmonizes with the Epistle as a whole.

Throughout the Epistle the writer shows that he
is expounding a religion which he, and those who
receive it, have been taught through authoritative
channels. He never uses the words of a founder of
the faith. He introduces, with a prefatory phrase,
passages which we have in our Gospels, as, 'Remember the words of our Lord Jesus Christ' (chaps.
xiii., xlvi.). With a claim to be humble followers of
the apostles, he and his fellow-members base their
faith on the teaching of our New Testament Epistles.[1]

We have dwelt upon this letter because it is the
most remarkable of extra-canonical Christian books.
It was regularly read in the meetings of the Church
of Corinth on Sundays (A.D. 170) a hundred years
after it was written; and we read that the Corinthians were about to do the same with another
Roman letter received at this later date. Nothing
could be more natural, at least as regards Clement's
letter (Euseb. *II. E.* iv. 23). No sermon of a local
preacher was likely to be more edifying than that
ancient letter, so full of wisdom and love. This
local partiality quite accounts in such a case—and
such cases must have been many—for an Epistle
being read in a particular Church though it did
not receive and did not claim canonical position or
apostolic authority. There is no trace of canonical
authority having been granted to this, the earliest
and best of the writings of the apostolic fathers.

[1] See *Ign. ad Philad.* chap. vii. for similar claim.

It was read in Corinth. But the mere fact that another letter written and received in the end of the second century was read in Corinth along with it, shows that the public reading of it did not imply its being regarded as Scripture. It was a valuable letter, and was frequently read elsewhere than in Corinth. It was so much liked that it was eventually written out and appended to the New Testament. We find it in mss.; we find it in lists of New Testament books. We are speaking of a later date, however. In the earliest days of the Church it was not so. It was never counted a competitor with our canonical books for general recognition; and when it did find a place in a kind of appendix to the New Testament, there was found along with it a homily by an unknown author,— the earliest extant Christian sermon by an uninspired man,—curiously termed the 'Second Epistle of Clement,' but of no canonical worth. We conclude, as regards 'Clement's Epistle,' that it does not really claim inspiration or authority, but that the fact of there being two ambiguous phrases in it which possibly were interpreted as making such a claim, may have helped it to find general acceptance throughout the Church.

ᴗ The so-called 'Second Epistle of Clement' is of doubtful age and authorship. It has only been found of late in a complete form; and now that it is all in our hands, we see that it is

a sermon or homily addressed to a Christian con-
gregation. There is no reason to connect it with
Clement, though, upon the whole, it may be
regarded as a sermon preached in Corinth, and in
this way locally associated with Clement's Epistle,
so as to be like it habitually read, along with the
New Testament, in ordinary services of worship.
It is singularly interesting as a specimen of
Christian preaching, as the oldest uninspired
Christian sermon now extant. We learn from it
of what sort some of the earliest preaching was.
We see little teaching of what we call doctrine,
—the relation of the different parts of Christian
truth to each other, — but there is, nevertheless, a strong hold of the essential verities
of the faith, and an unsparing assault on the
prevalent error of the times, which, starting from
the Gnostic tenet of the essential sinfulness of
matter, went on to deny the resurrection of the
body, and to minimize the sinfulness of fleshly
lusts. The preacher eloquently and affectionately
urges his hearers to consider the greatness of the
present life, on the ground that in it Christ's salvation must be accomplished in every one of us.
He makes no claim of inspiration or of authority
for himself; he calls the Scriptures the Word
of the 'God of Truth;' and though he quotes
apocryphal books, both of the Old Testament
and of the New, there is nothing to make us

regard him as more than a powerful and, on the whole, a useful preacher of those Christian truths which he himself calls the 'oracles of God.'

Still more clear is the absence of canonical claim or canonical recognition in the case of 'Barnabas.' The Epistle which bears the name of Paul's comrade cannot be accepted as his, because of the writer's amazing ignorance of the things of Israel, and because of his exaggerated statements as to the abandoned sinfulness of the apostles before they were 'called.' It seems to have been written about A.D. 120, its clear dependence on John's Gospel preventing our giving it the earlier date of A.D. 71 or A.D. 72, which some scholars have favoured. It was much thought of during the third century, both Clement of Alexandria and Origen treating it with marked respect. Clement calls it 'apostolic,' and Origen calls it 'catholic.' Yet neither of them can be justly charged with including it in the New Testament. And no one else went so near to that as they did. Does the writer, then, claim to have a place in the world of letters beside the great Apostle of the Gentiles? On the contrary, the whole tone of the Epistle is that of a man of little knowledge, and unduly proud of that little, but never speaking as though he were an authority. Not only this, but he is the first outside of the Canon to refer to the New Testament as to a written and authoritative record. '*It is written,*

Many are called, but few chosen' (chap. iv.). This
is not an accidental expression. It occurs in a
long passage making use of St. Matthew's Gospel,
and it is a distinct reference to the New Testament,
with the same kind of deference as was usually
paid to the Old. The writer was not indebted to
Matthew alone. His thought and his theology
clearly prove that he had drunk deeply at the
sources in the Gospel and Epistles of John. The
teaching of Peter and Paul and James may also
be traced in the Epistle (chap. viii.). There is
only one quotation from an Old Testament
apocryphal book. Here, then, we have a book in
high esteem, which not only does not claim to be
Scripture, but quotes the gospel as Scripture.

The next of the writings of apostolic fathers
found along with New Testament books in the
esteem of some authors and in some MSS., is the
'Shepherd' of Hermas, a curious, mystical book,
dating from about the year A.D. 142. Of the personality of the author, save that he had a brother,
Pius who was Bishop of Rome, we know absolutely
nothing. Whether he was old or young when the
second century began, whether he had ever seen
the city and the temple in which walked Christ's
blessed feet, we cannot tell, though all the indications
of the work itself point to a later date. It is easier
to learn the history of John Bunyan from the
Pilgrim's Progress, than to guess at the experiences

of Hermas from his book. But this much we can
say, that he nowhere claims any right to be regarded
as an inspired teacher, though the partiality of some
of the later Christian writers magnified his position
so as to credit him with inspiration. Clement of
Alexandria ascribes a divine origin to the words of
Hermas, and often quotes him. Origen says that he
was divinely inspired, and the generous eclecticism
of those two great Alexandrian teachers led them
to acknowledge the divine gift in all good things
said by good men ; but be it observed that neither
of them gave the book a place in Holy Scripture.
The wide admission of inspiration is one thing, the
recognition of authoritative Scripture is another
and very different thing. An early document,
called the Muratorian Fragment, written soon after
the work of Hermas, says the 'Shepherd' must
never to the end of time be reckoned with prophets
or apostles, or be publicly read to the people in the
Church. The writer's own claim is, that he en-
forces the moral precepts of the gospel on those
who accepted its facts and doctrines. The book is
an attempt to persuade Christians, by allegory and
similitude, to walk worthy of the vocation wherewith they had been called.

There is one other early writer—Polycarp—
earlier than the so - called Barnabas, almost as
early as Clement, who was the pupil of the
apostles, and who had the special distinction of

being the beloved disciple of the beloved Apostle
John.   He lived to a great old age, though he
died in the end a martyr's death.   His short
letter, whose genuineness has not been success-
fully impugned, is as rich in quotation and
reference, as full of the spirit of the New Testament, as though it were the work of Archbishop
Leighton.   Peter and Paul and John—we find him
speak in the words and thoughts of all those great
apostles.   We find him teaching what he had been
taught ;. but instead of asserting for himself any
right to stand on the same platform with those
pillars of the Church, he explicitly defines his
position to be that of a humble and unworthy
follower.   He is writing to the Philippians at their
request, and he says : 'Do we not know that the
saints shall judge the world, as Paul teaches ?   But
I have neither seen nor heard of any such thing
among you, in the midst of whom the blessed Paul
laboured, and who are such as he commends in the
beginning of his Epistle.   For he boasts of you in
all those churches which alone then had known the
Lord, but we [of Smyrna] had not yet known Him.'

Nor is this all.   The aged saint was in real
alarm lest men should over-estimate him because in
his youth he had sat at the feet of John, and was in
the habit of recounting anecdotes of the later years
of the disciple who had lain on the Saviour's breast.[1]

---

[1] See Irenæus' Letter to Florinus: Stieren's *Irenæus*, i. 823.

H

For this end he elaborately discredits himself, that he may refer the men of Philippi to the apostle whom the Spirit sent 'over to help' them in the beginning of the gospel.

Nor is even this all. As I have remarked elsewhere,[1] the whole Epistle is an exposition of documents accepted as standard and authoritative. The word *Canon* was not yet in use with its present meaning ; but the whole attitude of Polycarp is that of one who was interpreting accepted Scriptures. 'It is not Polycarp as a man who speaks, but a fellow-sinner and fellow-Christian, who has no right nor title to address them, save in so far as God gives him grace to remind them of the revealed word, which in his own experience he has found to be true and precious beyond all price.' This Epistle, then, is no competitor for a canonical place, but it is a valuable testimony to our Canon.

'These things, brethren, I write unto you concerning righteousness, not because I take anything upon myself, but because you have invited me to do so.

'*For neither I nor any one else like me can come up to the wisdom of the blessed and glorified Paul.* He, when among you, accurately and stedfastly taught the word of truth in the presence of those who were then alive. And when absent from you, he wrote

---

[1] *Canonicity*, p. 39.

you a letter which, if you carefully study, you will find to be the means of building you up in that faith which has been given you, and which, being followed by hope, and preceded by love towards God and Christ, and our neighbours, is the mother of us all. For if any one be inwardly possessed of those graces, he hath fulfilled the command of righteousness, since he that hath love is far from all sin.'

'Ignatius' is another of the apostolic fathers whom it is usual to cite. If the Epistles were really those of Ignatius, there could be nothing more interesting. The saint of Antioch is being carried to Rome to be the prey of the lions; and while he is thus dragged across the Asiatic continent to be butchered in Rome's bloody holiday, he addresses letters from various halting-places to churches and individuals that were near his heart. Fifteen letters run in his name: some think only seven of them are genuine, either in the shorter or in the longer form (for we have a choice); some insist upon the genuineness of only three. If any of the forms of those letters were genuine, we should have New Testament quotations enough for many purposes. We could prove the existence of the New Testament, the supreme power of the Episcopal hierarchy, the High Church sacramental theories, and other things besides. But when we could prove so much, we distrust the proof. We

neither doubt the story of Ignatius, nor the fact
that his real letters were the kernel of what
bears his name; but they have been so altered
and interpolated, especially as regards quotations
from the New Testament, and their original
form seems so utterly irrecoverable, that we
cannot found anything upon any specific expression
contained in them. Those letters, therefore, lie
outside of our argument. If they were accepted,
they would prove that at the time of Ignatius, disputants in the Christian Church appealed to written
standards (*ad Philad.* viii.); nay, it might appear
that one part of the New Testament was known as
'the Gospel,' and another as the testimony of the
'apostles' (*Ibid.* i. 5). At all events, it would be
clear beyond a doubt that the writer bent not only
with reverence but with superstitious fear before the
writers and the rulers of the Church which Christ
had founded.[1] I am aware that, in declining to
accept his testimony, I am turning away from one
who would be a powerful witness. But in the
search for truth we can have no help save from
what is true.

One other testimony of quite a different kind
comes to us from those early days. Its author is no
preacher like Clement, no amplifier of the theology
of Paul like Polycarp, but a caterer of traditions, a

---

[1] *Ign. ad. Philad.* chap. viii., claims for the writer God's guiding
grace; but any Christian may claim that God keeps him from being
deceived by those whose arguments are 'according to the flesh.'

man who went about, note-book in hand, to pick up
what fell from those who had seen the apostles and
immediate disciples of the Lord Jesus.   This busy
taker of notes, Papias, bishop of Hierapolis, wrote
five books of 'Exposition of the Oracles of the Lord.'
They have perished, save a few scraps, which are
embalmed in quotations of a later time.   He seems
to have collected what appeared to him to be the
most important sayings and doings of Christ, and to
have appended to each of them a commentary, sometimes enforcing the moral of the divine precept,
sometimes furnishing an illustration of the truth
from the experiences and the statements of the
worthies of the earlier time.   Papias lived from
about A.D. 70 to A.D. 150, and long laboured at his
vocation.   Some of the apostles he seems to have
met.   John was his teacher and Polycarp his
comrade, the daughters of Philip were his contemporaries, and in his own maturer years he was
the associate of many who had met more of the
founders of the Church than it had been his own
lot to meet.   Altogether he was an authority
on what had taken place, or had been believed, in
Asia Minor.

And what, then, says Papias ?   Does he set up
his book as a rival or an equal of the Gospels, to
the existence of which he testifies ?   On the contrary, few as are the fragments of his work which
have come down to us, it is evident from them that

he fulfilled his function when he preserved traditions about the authoritative books of the New Testament. He says that Mark compiled his Gospel from his notes of the preaching of Peter, whose companion he was.[1] It has in Papias' eyes all the authority due to a faithful transcript of the teaching of Peter. He tells us also that Matthew wrote his account of the divine oracles in Hebrew, and that there was at first no authorized translation from the Hebrew. Like one who accompanies pilgrims through a fair land, and who stops at each monument or striking feature of the landscape, confirming by his appropriate lore the impression which those well-known features make on the observant mind, Papias entertains those who, like himself, reverenced the Gospels and honoured the departed apostles, with his reminiscences of the books and the men that were the landmarks of the new Christian life. He says : ' I shall not refuse to arrange for you along with my interpretations [of Scripture] those things also which in former days I well learned from the elders and well recorded, being myself well assured of the truth concerning them. For I was not like most people, prone to find my chief pleasure in those who furnished ordinary conversation, but I found my delight in those who were teaching the things that are true; nor did I attach myself to those who

---

[1] This ancient testimony is confirmed or repeated by many later writers. (See Moesinger's edition of Ephrem's *Com.* on Tatian's *Dia-tessaron.* Ephrem adds that Mark was written in Latin.)

recorded the precepts of people with whom we have no concern, but to those who told of the precepts which were given by the Lord for the nourishment of faith, and who came to us after being near to the Truth Himself. So, then, when any one came who had been an associate of the elders, I inquired at him about the elders' words,—what Andrew or what Peter said, or what Philip said, or Thomas, or James, or John, or Matthew, or any other of the disciples of the Lord, or what Aristion and the Presbyter John, the disciples of the Lord, are saying in our own time. For I was not in the way of supposing that I was so much indebted to things out of books as to those which came from the living and abiding voice.'

There is some ambiguity in those last words, disparaging books, if they are taken by themselves; but when read along with the context, they mean that for his purpose of traditional illustration, the chief source of information was the conversation of men who had seen the Lord and those who once were His companions. He lived in a time of much speaking; he lived in a commercial district, where many men had much to say of what they had seen; and around him were in circulation books of every kind, books of philosophy, or of philosophic commentary on the New Testament Scriptures; but with a sly hit at their wordiness, he turned away from all those to pursue his own definite purpose.

There is no small probability that in this last
part of the account of his work Papias was referring to the wordy works of his Gnostic contemporaries, whose systems were plentiful, copious, and
shortlived as mushrooms. A Syrian contemporary
of his, Basilides by name, wrote no fewer than
twenty-four books upon the gospel, of the nature
of which a learned man like Papias—for Eusebius,
who loved him little, tells us that he was a man
of much lore—must have been well aware. Taken
in this sense, his words mean that he found it more
profitable to listen to those who had some actual
fact to tell, than to those who wrote long-winded
speculations upon the doctrine of Christ.

This, at least, is abundantly certain, that Papias
never dreamed of his chronicles and memorials
and illustrations being set up alongside the works
of the apostles and of those whom they guided in
writing. His work was no rival of the canonical
books.

The reference of Papias to the wordiness of his
contemporaries leads us to turn to the Gnostics,
who, as we have just said, were the most
voluminous authors of his day. Their position
was one of antagonism to the ordinary teaching
of the Church. The testimonies we have hitherto
considered belong to the orthodox Church ; and
it might be supposed that some rivals to the
ordinary standards of doctrine in the Church would

emerge in the great Gnostic systems of the first
and second centuries.   Yet it is not so.

For those Gnostics were men who claimed to
have knowledge, and who sought it through human
philosophy, but yet did not give up their adherence
to the simple verities of Christianity.   The staple
of the teaching in the Ep. - Apostolic Church,
as we may infer from the homily known as
Clement's 'Second Epistle,' was not doctrine, but
an outline of the facts of the life of Jesus, and an
enforcement of the great ethical lessons of purity
and peace which could be deduced from these facts.
But such plain facts did not suit the Greeks, who
' sought after wisdom,' or the Orientals, whose
giants of thought had long speculated on the
origin of good and evil, of mind and matter.   In
the great towns of Greece and Asia Minor, above
all in Alexandria, where Judaism and heathen
philosophy had long been blended, philosophers
who became Christians were under some constraint
to combine the gospel with their philosophy.   And
to them, therefore, doctrine was everything.   They
were well aware that their doctrine was not like
that which prevailed in the Church.   They were
proud of having passed beyond the limits of 'faith,'
as ordinarily understood, and of expatiating in the
wide field of ' knowledge.'   They were not content
to have their horizon in the life of Jesus or in the
mountains of Israel ; they still had an Evangelic

Record for their centre ; but for the origin of all
things they went back to the primeval thought of
God, and for the end of all they looked to the fulfil-
ment of the promise that evil should be led into
captivity by Christ, and all things in heaven and
earth be reconciled to God in Him.

The remarkable result of all this was that, instead
of decrying the sacred writings, they magnified
them.   It was their aim to proceed from the
starting-point of the revelation which they found in
the New Testament, and to advance to what they
believed to be the highest attainments of Christian
philosophy.   Their writings often obscured the
truth ; but they possessed it, and I have no doubt
honestly strove to expound it, and to make it the
core of their speculations.   They tortured, twisted,
and diluted it, until its spirit was quite gone, but
all the more on that account did they magnify the
value of its 'letter.'   What books they actually
manufactured—many of them known as the New
Testament Apocrypha—were avowedly supplementary to our Gospels.   Not even one of them could
be a substitute.   The Apocryphal Gospels take up
portions of the life of Jesus which our four Evangelists have left untold, or they enforce some
subordinate doctrine for which the New Testament
gives no authority.   The oldest and best of the
Apocryphal Gospels, known as the Gospel of James,
tells of the parentage of the mother of Jesus and

her perpetual dignity; another — the Gospel of
Thomas—tells marvellous stories of the Redeemer's
childhood; another, which is known as part of the
Gospel of Nicodemus, is an account of Christ's
doings in the under world while His body was in
Joseph's tomb. The Apocryphal 'Acts' are each
designed to solve some knotty question of doctrine
or of church government. But all of them suppose
the existence of canonical books, of which they are
echoes, expansions, satellites. And they are all
indirect but distinct confirmations of the tradition
of the Church regarding the early origin and
authority of the canonical books.

But it behoved the Gnostics to commend their
systems of philosophy by showing how they could
be reconciled with the words of Scripture. And the
first Canon of New Testament Scripture was compiled by a Gnostic—Marcion; the first commentary
on the words of any part of Scripture was written
by a Gnostic—Heracleon; and the oldest professed
homilies or commentaries on the doctrines of the
gospel were written by another and earlier Gnostic
—Basilides. In the Christian Church, yet scarcely
of it, those early philosophers are valuable witnesses to the books of the New Testament; for
they set up no avowed rivals, they wished only
to expound or to commend the accepted books.

The Christian congregations in those days had
no minute systems of doctrine; the broad outlines

of truth and duty sufficed for them; and in many cases the exact words of Scripture were of small account.   Just because they followed the true tradition of true doctrine, they were often not learned in the letter.   And just because the Gnostics left that tradition, they had to plead the letter as their warrant.   It was therefore they—and not the orthodox—that first established the principles of canonicity.

We shall see this if we look at typical Gnostic work in the regions of *philosophy, criticism,* and *imagination.*

Basilides is the philosopher whom we take as an example of the way in which Gnostics made it their business to weave Scripture words into the terminology of their systems.

We have already spoken of him as the author of a voluminous work on the gospel.   He flourished as an influential teacher about A.D. 125 in Egypt, Syria, and perhaps Persia.   He had meditated on John's teaching, that all things were made by the Logos; he had longed for the realizing of Paul's teaching, that the universe is reconciled to God in Jesus Christ; and we find him quoting our Gospels, and labouring to show how the groaning creation shall one day be set free, and how the true Light will lighten every man that cometh into the world.   But in strange contrast with this noble aim seems to be his

system, at all events when its skeleton or abstract
is set before us.   From the supreme God came
forth in the primeval eternity the germ of all
things, an egg, in which, if we may use a
modern phrase, was 'the promise and potency
of all life;' and out of this egg, in necessary
development, grew the principalities and powers
which Jesus the Archon's Son is to enlighten as
Saviour and Light.   Anxiously did Basilides
quote John's prologue, and weave in words
from Colossians and Ephesians.   Thus did he
profess to set greater store on New Testament
writings than those whose simple life of faith was
moulded by them.   But this was not even all.
He tried to lay hold of the current reverence for
oral tradition in the Church; he claimed to have
had the benefit of the oral teaching of a certain
Glaucias, who had been Peter's pupil, and to have
the true doctrine of Matthias, whom Jesus Himself
instructed.   In answer to every assault on his
system as being contrary to the words of sound
doctrine on which men had grown up, he would
quote some text of the New Testament that could
be forced to support him.   Thus was Basilides,
though a perverter of the gospel, a maintainer of
the writings of the founders of the Church.

His testimony is especially important in the
evidence for the early date and apostolic authorship of John's Gospel.   In the recently discovered

treatise, which is commonly accepted as the
'Refutation of all Heresies' by Hippolytus, and
as dating about A.D. 220, is an account of Basilides
and his followers. In course of this account there
occur two remarkable passages with quotations
from John's Gospel. We may here quote them,
as showing how this ancient Gnostic laboured at
his task of constructing a Christian cosmogony :—

'But since it was incompetent to say that any projection of a
non-existent God became a non-existent something,—for Basilides
altogether shuns and dreads existences beginning in projection,
— for what kind of emanation would thus be needed, or what
material must be posited, that God might make the world
as a spider makes his threads, or as some mortal man takes
brass, or wood, or some other material for his craft? ——
. . . From things non-existent, he says, came into being the
seed of the world, viz. the word which was spoken: "Let there
be light;" and this, he says, is that which is said in the Gospels:
"That was the true Light, which lighteth every man on his
coming into the world."'[1]

That those words refer to John's Gospel no one
can deny. But some deny that Basilides wrote
them. Yet are they at the heart of the Basilidian
system; and what Basilidian would have been in
Hippolytus' eye save the founder of the system
himself? Isidore, his son, is out of the question.
He did not quote Scripture in that way, so far as
we know. And we hold them for the words of
Basilides, the more so that Basilides is specially

[1] Hippol. *Ref. Hær.* vii. 22, p. 360 (Duncker and Schneidewin's
edition). See *Canonicity*, p. 173.

named in the immediately preceding words, and
is known to have accepted our Gospels.

There is another passage which shows the
acquaintance of the philosopher with our Gospels :

'And, says he, that each one has his special times the Saviour
Himself is a competent witness when He says: "My time is not
yet come." And the Magi who gazed at [His] star are witnesses [that there is a fixed hour]: For, says he, He Himself
[*i.e.* Jesus] was appointed beforehand at the time of the birth of
stars, and of the times of restitution in the great universe.'[1]

We now turn to the *critical* Gnostic.

Marcion, the representative of Gnostic criticism,
came some ten years after Basilides ; and from
A.D. 135 his views were widely spread in Rome
and Syria. He was from Pontus, on the shores
of the Black Sea. Basilides had been content to
accept the gospel narrative substantially as it
stood (Hippol. *Ref. Hær.* iii. 27 ; see *Can.* p. 49),
and to found his system upon a philosophy which
transmuted Scriptural simplicity into Gnostic
speculation ; but Marcion undertook a harder task.
Like most Gnostics, he believed that matter is
essentially evil; that the God of the Old Testament
is the Creator of matter or the representative of its
evil power; and that Jesus Christ came to establish
a new dispensation in entire antagonism to the
system of the Old Testament.

Starting with an exaggerated view of St. Paul's

[1] Hippol. vii. 27 ; *Canonicity,* p. 173.

opposition to the law, and so claiming Paul as an
opponent of the Old Testament, he gave forth
ten of Paul's Epistles[1] as the apostolical part of
his own New Testament, and he adopted them
with little change.   His doing this shows how
little knowledge or study of doctrine there was in
the Church at his time ; because it is impossible
to reconcile such Epistles as Romans or Galatians
with his system.   But it was not in those doctrinal
books that Marcion found the strength of his
position.   It was in the life of the Saviour.   Jesus
Christ, the Way, and the Truth, and the Life, was
the centre of the theology of the Church ; and
Marcion must needs have a Gospel to confirm his
heretical views of the Redeemer's work.

The way he accomplished this is unparalleled
in his time.   We have said—speaking generally—
that none of the books which originated in the
early Church were rivals of our canonical Gospels.
Marcion's was a rival, but in such a way as to
show how secure was the position of the Gospels
before his time.   Marcion did not dare to make
a Gospel.   He could not palm off a new one,
but he thought he might alter one of the Gospels
already in use ; and he took the Gospel of Luke
and audaciously mutilated it to suit his purpose.
He omitted all reference to the Baptist as the fore-

---

[1] The Pauline Epistles, with the omission of those to the Hebrews
and to Timothy and Titus.

runner of the Christ, because he could not allow
that a man of the Old Testament could be on the
same side as the Saviour; he omitted all reference
to the nativity and birth of Jesus, because he
could not admit that Christ came in the flesh—
that flesh which, in his view, was of its own
nature evil; and he made it appear that the
Supreme God came suddenly down in human guise,
though not in human flesh, to the synagogues of
Capernaum.   On through all the narrative[1] the
same policy is pursued by this critic; and there
is no doubt that we have in Marcion's work a
proof of the supreme position of our canonical
Gospel in the Church.   It is ample proof that the
heretic's only hope of a basis for his Gnosticism
was in mutilating one of the books to which all
men looked up with reverence and love.   The
mutilation was so consistent, so thorough, and
yet the changes were in themselves so slight,—a
few words dropped out, or one word slightly
changed, and the thing was done,—that Marcion
hoped the simple - minded would not see how
complete was the revolution his sacrilegious
hand effected.   But after all that he did, his
system can be refuted from the passages he
left, and from the Epistles, which he strangely
omitted to cut down; so that one still feels the

---

[1] See *Canonicity*, pp. 393–410, for a full account of Marcion, of
the chief mutilations made by him on the Gospel of Luke, and of the
reasons which probably moved him to the mutilation in each case.

I

vigorous Tertullian to have been right when
he said: 'Marcion, I pity thee. Thy labour is
in vain; for my Jesus Christ still remains in thy
Gospel.'

We now turn to look at Gnosticism in the regions
of *imagination*. In doing so we have to name
Gnostics of an earlier time. Of Simon Magus,
'the hero of the romance of heresy,' with which we
have to do, and the reputed founder of Gnosticism,
we know very little that can be relied upon. But
what we do know shows that he had attempted to
make a cosmogony, of which the central tenet was
that the material creation is the result of the
degradation of a thought of God; and that all
manifestations of the Supreme God, whether as
Father, Son, or Holy Spirit, were designed to set
that captive thought of God free from its fetters.
Simon himself claimed to be the mighty manifestation of God, the impersonation of the Holy Spirit;
'the great power of God,' said his partisans in
Samaria; and no other Gnostic dared, as he seems
to have done, thus to set himself above Jesus Christ.
Succeeding ages kept him in mind; but we should
hear little of him were it not for a strange Romance
which has come down to us from about the middle
of the second century, with Simon for its hero. It
is known in two forms, as the 'Clementine Homilies'
(in Greek) and the 'Recognitions of Clement' (in
Latin). An early Judaeo-Christian set himself to

exalt Simon Peter and the Jewish party in the
Christian Church; and under the form of an
autobiography of a rich young man, Clement by
name, who had lost his means and his family, and
who followed the fortunes and recorded the sermons
of Peter, we have a sharp contrast between the
teachings of Peter and those of Simon Magus. It
is not possible to overlook the fact that some of
the positions said to be maintained by Simon are
really those of Paul. Paul's greatness is shown
by the fact that the writer never dares to name him.
At the same time, the speculations and the story
of Simon himself are recorded in parts of the
strange farrago, and we are often reminded of the
collision between Simon and the apostles of which
we are told by St. Luke (Acts viii.). As the
narrative proceeds the conflict deepens, until at
last righteousness triumphs, the lost parents of
Clement are found, and the truth is established
by miracle and judgment.

It has been attempted to find in this book the
canonical book of the Judæo-Christian party in the
Church. But more deliberate study has, I believe,
dissipated this idea. The work has none of the
characteristics of a book to be regarded as Scripture. It supposes that its readers or hearers are
familiar with the Old Testament, and also with
the Gospel narrative. It is a polemical work,
treating all Scripture, Old Testament and New,

with great freedom; but the materials thus mani-
pulated can for the most part be found in our
Bibles.   There are only three or four sayings[1]
ascribed to Christ which we do not find in our New
Testament; and while their actual source is not
known, they are such as might well be found in
oral tradition.   We do not care to deny the possibility of their being drawn from some apocryphal
or extra-canonical gospel, but we can say that no
one knows what it is.   On the other hand, there
are quotations from Matthew, many, clear, and
detailed; Mark is unquestionably used; and not
only are there allusions to Luke, but there are
quotations from John.

The history of this last piece of evidence as to the
use of the fourth Gospel is singular.   It forms
one of several recent discoveries which have helped
to make the evidence of the reception of the New
Testament Scripture clearer than in former days.
When Baur promulgated his famous theory of the
gradual growth of the New Testament and of the
recent date of the fourth Gospel, he and his followers exalted the antiquity and value of the
Clementines, and pointed to their independence of
our Gospels, and to the absence of any definite
quotation from the fourth Gospel.   While their
date was carried back to the middle of the century,

---

[1] *Hom.* iii. 50, 55, xix. 20, and perhaps xii. 2. See *Canonicity*,
p. lxvii.

John's Gospel was supposed not to have been publicly known until about A.D. 160. When Baur wrote, the Homilies (or Greek form) of the Clementines were not complete. But when the complete manuscript was published by Dressel, A.D. 1853, it was found that there was in the previously unknown portion (*Hom.* xix. 22) a quotation from the account of the healing of the blind man in John's Gospel. However early, therefore, may be the date of the Homilies, by so much the earlier is the testimony to the public position of John's Gospel. It is not only that this one reference to the blind man is found, but its indisputable existence enables us to put due weight on some other less distinct allusions, so that we can now find frequent traces of the fourth Gospel in this strange Romance.[1] To the Epistles of Paul there is no undoubted reference, and this makes the apparent assault on St. Paul's views the more perplexing. Paul's views were, of course, well known long before this time, and it is curious to see how they are denounced without being stated. . But whatever may have been the theology of the author of the Clementine story, the whole texture of the book shows its unfitness to be the Scripture of any sect. It is the work of an individual expressing the prejudices of a section of the community ; and its wordy, irrelevant, and complicated

---

[1] The necessity of regeneration (*Hom.* xi. 26). 'I am the door of the sheep. My sheep hear my voice' (*Hom.* iii. 52) ; and also John viii. 44, compared with *Hom.* iii. 25.

discussions are incapable of furnishing guidance to any one who desires to stand in an intelligent relation to Christianity.

The foregoing are three Gnostics whom we may take as types. But of the Gnostics as a whole we may say that they tend to confirm the position of the canonical books. Some of them might reject one part and some another of the complete Christian doctrine, but more usually they exaggerated an undoubted truth. Thus Simon, when he claimed that he was the Great Incarnation,[1] showed that he adopted the central fact of Christianity—God manifest in the flesh; when Cerinthus,[2] and such as he, regarded the material world as the work of beings inferior to the Great God, he showed his conviction that the revelation of the Supreme One was the glory of the Christian era, for that the Great God is nearer to man than He had ever been before Christ came; and even the Naassenes or Ophites,[3] who declared that Cain and the Sodomites had been the champions of oppressed truth, were led to their grotesque heresies by a desire to show how much better, brighter, and broader is the revelation in the New Testament than men had ever dreamed of before.

Thus up to the middle of the second century we have found that our New Testament is the centre

---

[1] See *Canonicity*, p. 383.   [2] See *Canonicity*, p. 384.
[3] See *Canonicity*, p. 385, and note; see also p. 388.

of life alike in the orthodox Church and in the Gnostic sects outside of it.[1]

---

[1] On the Gnostics as connected with the apocryphal books time does not permit us to speak fully here. See the chapter 'Apocryphal Literature' in *Canonicity*, Introduct. p. cviii. The 'Gospel of James,' 'Acts of Paul and Thecla,' and 'Acts of Pilate,' all testify to the books of the New Testament. The first two are probably of the first century; the last is of uncertain age in its present form.

LECTURE V.

EVIDENCE OF THE APOLOGISTS, VERSIONS, AND CHRISTIAN
WRITERS, FROM JUSTIN MARTYR TO EUSEBIUS.

WE have traced the testimonies to the Canon
through the Gnostics till the second quarter of the
second century was well begun.   But we must
now come back from those collateral witnesses to
consult the writers who may be regarded as in the
direct line of the Church.   The period from A.D.
130 to A.D. 170 is remarkable as an era of Apologics.
The Apologists were men who defended Christians
rather than Christianity against the prejudices and
assaults of both the vulgar and the leaders of Rome.
They were concerned to make it clear that heathen
rulers would be well advised if they allowed Christians to live undisturbed in the practice of their
religion, inasmuch as, in consequence of adopting
that religion, they led better lives, and were therefore more useful citizens than the other subjects of
the empire.   Justin Martyr was the first whose
writings have come down to us.   Quadratus, Aris-
tides, and Agrippa Castor were older, but their
writings have perished.[1]   Justin challenges all men

---

[1] See *Canonicity*, p. 66, note.

to apply the test of a good and useful life to the disciples of Jesus Christ as compared with any or all of
their heathen neighbours. He shows how their recognition of obligations to a spiritual God and to a
holy Saviour led to their being chaste, peace-loving,
honourable in business, obedient to rulers ; and he
shows that, instead of practising horrible secret
rites, as vulgar gossip would have it, they had a
worship which was simple and pure, naturally fitting
them for works of mutual charity and helpfulness.
' We continually remind ourselves of these things,
and the wealthy among us help the needy, and we
always keep together ; and for all things wherewith
we are supplied we bless the Maker of all, through
His Son Jesus Christ, and through the Holy
Spirit.'[1] It was to be expected that such Apologies
or defences, being addressed to heathen, would not
quote the sacred books in the same way as would
have been natural in exhorting Christians. But not
only is there an absence of quotation, there is ab-

---

[1] Peregrinus burned himself about A.D. 165. His story (which illus-
trates Justin) is told us by his contemporary Lucian, a mocking heathen,
the registrar of Alexandria, to this effect :—In prison, men came from
the cities of Asia to minister to him. ' Not being able to effect his
release, they did him all kinds of offices, and that not in a careless
manner, but with the greatest assiduity ; for even betimes in the morning
there would be at the prison old women, some widows, and also orphan
children ; and some of the chief of their men, by corrupting the keepers,
would get into prison and stay the whole night with him, and there
they had a good supper together, and their sacred discourses. . . .
It is incredible what expedition they use when any of their friends are
known to be in trouble. In a word, they spare nothing upon such an
occasion ; and Peregrinus' claim brought him in a good sum of money
from them ; for these miserable men have no doubt that they shall be

solutely no case of their naming the Gospels in connection with the authors.[1] Justin sets the example ;
his disciple Tatian follows it in his ‘ Oration to the
Gentiles ;’ and even Tertullian, though on other
occasions he is most profuse and minute in his
quotations, when he is writing his ‘ Apology’ never
names the Gospels. Nor does even Cyprian at a
later date, when the books were familiarly known
to all. The truth is that in those times Christians
had not so much call to prove to heathen what
books were their standards, as to show what manner
of men they were in daily life. And one cannot read
those old defences of the religion of Christ without
feeling how perilous it would be in many respects
to challenge heathen enemies to apply to us in these
days the practical tests which were invited in the
second century. Justin himself is an instance of
the power of the lives of Christians over fair
observers. He had tried in his youth the Peripatetic and the Pythagorean philosophy for comfort,
but in vain. He next turned to Platonism, and
‘ such was my stupidity,’ he says, ‘ that I expected
forthwith to look upon God, for this is the end of

immortal and live for ever, therefore they contemn death, and many of
them surrender themselves. Moreover, their first lawgiver has taught
them that they are all brethren. . . . They have a sovereign contempt for all things of this world, and look upon them as common,
and trust one another with them without any particular security, for
which reason any subtle fellow may by good management impose upon
those simple people, and grow rich among them ’ (Lucian, *De Morte
Peregrini*, chap. xi. *Canonicity*, p. 368).

[1] See Norton, *Genuineness of the Gospels*, i. 137, for an eloquent passage.

Plato's philosophy.' In this mood he was when he found God by looking on good men, not by the exercise of Platonic meditation. ' For what man who is voluptuous, or who regards the eating of human flesh as an enjoyment [these were the vulgar charges against Christians], could welcome death with the certainty of being deprived of life's pleasures?' While thus touched with noble sympathy for Christ's disciples, he one day met a disciple who had grown grey in Christ's service, 'a meek and venerable man,' who told him that what Socrates and Plato despairingly longed for had actually come to pass, and that the living God had actually spoken to men by the Divine Spirit. The venerable Christian adjured him to pray that the gates of light might be opened to him. To Justin was immediately granted divine understanding, and he was soon possessed with a love of the prophets and of those men who are Christ's friends ; and he ' pondered these things in his mind,' and saw that Christianity is the only sure and fit philosophy. Full of faith and zeal, he travelled over the earth preaching the religion of Jesus. He died a noble death—the story of which is more pathetic because it reveals to us the Roman judge's inability to comprehend faith in the unseen, and a religion which needed no temple, than because it tells how a Christian won his crown.

Justin Martyr has not only left an Apology (or

two Apologies, if they be not parts of one), we have also from him a Dialogue with Trypho, a Jew; and we thus see how a Christian philosopher and teacher met the Gentile on the one hand and Israel on the other. This double relation would of itself give value to Justin's words; but in another double relation he is equally memorable. He stands midway between the Apostle John (A.D. 90–100), the last of the Evangelists, and Irenæus, bishop of Lyons (A.D. 180), in whose writings we find beyond all question the great bulk of our New Testament treated as canonical. Justin's Apology to the Emperor was presented about A.D. 140, so that we know the date of his full activity.

Forty years before, John had died in that city of Ephesus which was the scene of Justin's Dialogue; forty years later, Irenæus, who was Polycarp's scholar in Asia, perhaps in that same Ephesus, succeeded to the bishopric of Lyons. Nor is even this all that makes Justin remarkable. Being a native of Samaria, he was familiar with the life and work of another Samaritan, Simon Magus, the founder of Gnosticism. Being an enemy of Gnosticism, Justin wrote a treatise (now lost) against Marcion, his contemporary. 'And there is Marcion,' he says in his Apology, 'a native of Pontus, who is even at this day alive and teaching his disciples to believe in some other God greater than the Creator.' There may have met in Rome

some day Marcion, who made the first Canon by
binding together his edition of St. Luke's Gospel
and ten Epistles of St. Paul ; Valentinus, the founder
of a heresy which seized the minds of the people,
but who used our whole New Testament without
mutilation ; Tatian, who not only 'apologized'
for Christians to the emperor, but blended our
four Gospels in a Harmony ; and Justin Martyr
himself.

It may seem strange that Justin's testimony
should be so much more of a battle-ground than
that of any of those others. But a battle-
ground it has been for many a day ; though it
needs no prophet to see that the tide of war must
soon flow away from it, and leave it in possession
of orthodox Christians. Our older critics and
apologists confidently claimed him as a witness
for all our Gospels ; their recent followers,
especially in England, have been too timid to
take the same position ; but now they are taking
heart of grace again, as well they may.

What makes Justin's testimony difficult is that
instead of calling his authorities 'Gospels,' he
calls them 'Memoirs ;' either owing to some of
the classical affectations from which he was by no
means free, or perhaps because he thought that
his readers, who did not know the meaning of
'Gospels,' would understand the descriptive term
to denote that the books contained a historical

account of Christ. But it can be easily shown that Justin was quoting our Gospels all the while. He says that the 'Memoirs' on which he relies were written by apostles and their companions (words which remind us of St. Luke's preface); that they were publicly read in church along with the writings of the prophets ; that they contain full accounts of Jesus Christ,—nay, he on one occasion says they were 'called Gospels,' and at another time he refers to their substance or contents as 'the Gospel.'[1] His opponent, Trypho the Jew, admits having read them ; so that we know they were publicly accepted by friend and foe at that date as the authoritative books of the Christian faith.

It is quite true that he never quotes any one Gospel by name in his works still extant; but in appealing to a heathen there would have been little propriety in doing such a thing; and, as we have seen, no other Apologist did it any more than Justin. It is also true that in his argument with the Jew he uses some half-dozen[2] trifling apocryphal additions to the gospel narrative, but it is to be observed that he never says he got those things from the Memoirs. It is not less true that in his avowed quotations he almost confined himself to the *Jewish* Scriptures when

---

[1] See *Canonicity*, pp. 59–64.
[2] See the texts in *Canonicity*, p. 59.

arguing with Trypho; but every modern missionary
to the Jews must do the same, for thus only is
there common ground on which to go. The
Christian Memoirs are valuable, as containing
facts which fulfil those Jewish Scriptures, but the
Christian champion must quote them to a Jew as
history, not as Scripture. It is with the Gospels
Justin deals, not with St. Paul's Epistles,— as
indeed how could he in such a case?—nor with
any other books of the New Testament, save that
once in a formal and circuitous fashion he speaks
of the Apocalypse of John. It is true that he
does not always quote correctly—that his words
are not perfectly identical with those of our
Gospels. But they who on that account supply
him with another Gospel now lost,—the 'Gospel
of the Hebrews,' or such like,—must give him a
new copy even of his master, Plato, whom in
seven quotations he does not once quote correctly ;
and they must also suppose that he changed
even his Old Testament as well as his New,
because in more than half the cases when he
repeats a quotation, he changes some part of the
expression !

V It is almost incredible that on such slight
grounds as that a classical philosopher usually
called the books Memoirs (though once he called
them Gospels), and that he did not quote them
quite *verbatim*, some critics should for so long

have maintained that Justin did not know or did not acknowledge our Gospels. If this contention were well founded, it would follow that the books which Justin did know, and which were accepted in his day by Christian congregations and Jewish antagonists, disappeared, and were never more heard of — disappeared before even his disciple Tatian wrote a Harmony of four,—for Tatian's four are ours. As a matter of fact, we find Justin using each one of our Gospels. He uses the beginning of Matthew's Gospel, with its special information about the Magi; the opening of Luke, with its account of the mission of the angel to Mary ; Mark's Gospel, with its statement that the sons of Zebedee were Boanerges ; and John's, with its high teaching of the new birth, of the Word made flesh, of the living water, and of the heavenly habitations.

Hellenist by training though he was, he never even once quotes one of the Old Testament Apocrypha.

With the name of another of the Apologists, Justin's pupil, Tatian, has long been connected a certain mystery, because of the loss of his chief work, the *Diatessaron*, to which reference is made by Eusebius. During the reign of Marcus Aurelius, Tatian wrote an 'Oration to the Greeks,' in which are unmistakeable quotations from John's Gospel ;[1] but his Harmony being lost, and some

---

[1] See *Canonicity*, p. 180.

later stages of his life being chargeable with the promulgation of ascetic heresies, doubt has been thrown on his having used our four Gospels in making the Harmony. Two curious slips of ancient writers increased the perplexity; one by Victor of Capua, who says that he learned from Eusebius that Tatian wove together one Gospel out of the four, to which he attached the title of *Diapente* (*i.e.* of five) [instead of *Diatessaron* (*i.e.* of four)]; and another by Epiphanius, who says that some thought the *Diatessaron* was the Gospel of the Hebrews. Victor makes an obvious slip (1) because he gives as his authority Eusebius, who says no such thing; and (2) because his words contradict themselves, for nobody would give the name *Diapente* to a thing made of four. Epiphanius' words must remain as the outcome of one of his unfounded ideas, conceived and uttered on the impulse of a moment. Many other conjectures of scholars are proved to be baseless by a recent discovery, of which we must now speak.

One of the fathers of the Syrian Church in the fourth century, Ephrem by name, a critic, a theologian, and a poet, wrote a commentary on Tatian's *Diatessaron*, and that work has recently been discovered in an Armenian translation.[1] Ephrem does not quote all Tatian's text; but he quotes enough to show us that Tatian was not

[1] See note on Tatian's *Diatessaron* at the end of this chapter.

making what we call a Harmony, but was compiling a life of Christ — a Gospel — by weaving together the four Gospels of Matthew, Mark, Luke, and John.[1]   His title literally tells his plan.   It is 'By means of Four' — by means of the Four Evangelists—Tatian constructs the life of the Lord Jesus Christ.   His first paragraph is the prologue of John's Gospel: 'In the beginning was the Word;' and thus we see that at that time this scholarly Christian teacher had no more doubt of John than of the rest of the Evangelists.   On through the life of Jesus, Tatian pursues his plan, quoting now from one, now from another; the last chapter of John being woven into it, and allusion being made to the disputed verses in the end of Mark.   The close of the work is taken from Luke and the Acts, and tells of the disciples tarrying in Jerusalem till they should be endowed with power from on high.

It is not easy to exaggerate the importance of this, the most recent discovery in biblical literature. Like many discoveries illustrative of the Old Testament, this new work confirms the ordinary view of the Church as regards the age and authority of the books of Scripture.   Its importance is immense, for it not only proves that Tatian

[1] Zahn, in his *Forschungen zur Geschichte des N. T. Kanons*, 1 Theil., *Tatian's Diatessaron*, engages in the somewhat unprofitable task of fixing Tatian's text.

used our Gospels in making his work, but it necessarily throws back light upon the earlier quotations in Justin, in Basilides, and the rest, so as to show that even the fourth Gospel was not an invention of the second century,—as advanced critics would have led us to believe,—but was accepted at the very earliest times as the work of the beloved apostle himself.[1]

There are other Apologists, of whom, if time permitted, it would be right to speak in some detail. Any such detail would show that what we have seen to characterize Justin and Tatian is also found in the others. Their direct references to the New Testament are few; their defence of the character

---

[1] The author of *Supernatural Religion* will need to alter his text in regard to Tatian, as he had to alter it regarding Marcion. He says : ' There is, therefore, no authority for saying that Tatian's Gospel was a harmony of four Gospels at all. . . . Those who called the Gospel used by Tatian the Gospel according to the Hebrews must have read the work, and all that we know confirms their conclusion,' p. 158. Again, a little more boldly, he says: 'No one seems to have seen Tatian's Harmony, for the simple reason that there was no such work, and the real Gospel used by him was that according to the Hebrews, as many distinctly and correctly called it,' p. 160. Still more boldly he contradicts the Syrian tradition that Ephrem wrote a commentary on Tatian's Harmony, and concludes: 'All that we know of it [Tatian's Gospel], what it did not contain, the places where it largely circulated, and the name by which it was called, identifies it with the Gospel according to the Hebrews.' As his manner is, the learned author convinces himself by his own assertions, and what he states at first as a probability or as a necessity regarding Tatian's Harmony, becomes, ere he has done, a sheer assertion regarding Tatian's Gospel. He has wrought himself up to contradict the unvarying statement of antiquity that Tatian wrote a Harmony ; and to assert that only those spoke of it as a Harmony who did not know that it was the Gospel of the Hebrews. His probable loophole will be that what Ephrem commented on was the Harmony of Ammonius, not that of Tatian at all.

of Christians is explicit and ample. Thus Athenagoras, who, from the strange title of his work,
—An Embassy about Christians (πρεσβεια περὶ χρισ-
τιανῶν),—may be supposed to have presented it in
person to the Emperor Marcus Aurelius, names no
book, but refers to many, both gospels and epistles.
The wise man who then ruled the world must have
been impressed by the calm force with which
Athenagoras, 'Athenian philosopher and Christian,'
presented the case for the Christians.[1]

Melito of Sardis was a contemporary of Athenagoras ; a man of much industry, the very titles
of whose works (Euseb. *H. E.* iv. 26) show that
he wrote a library. About A.D. 170 or A.D. 176 he
presented his Apology, which seems to be lost,
though a kindred work of his comes to us through
the Syriac ; but a fragment of a letter he wrote to
a friend is interesting, as containing a list of the
Old Testament books, Esther excepted, which he
calls at one time ' the old books,' and at another
' the books of the Old Covenant.' From those
phrases we are entitled to infer that he recognised
certain ' new books,' or ' books of the New Covenant,'
on the same level with the old.[2]

Theophilus, another contemporary and apologist,
—for those days of the Antonines were the days
when Christianity was on its defence as a power in

---

[1] See *Canonicity*, p. 131.

[2] See *Canonicity*, p. 43, and Introduction, xci.

moulding the lives of the subjects of the Roman
Empire,—has the distinction of being the first
whom we find quoting the Gospel of John by name.
Before this time Heracleon, a Gnostic, had written
a commentary on that Gospel, but it has perished,
save what is embalmed in Origen. Theophilus'
work which remains is not an Apology addressed
to the Emperor, but a treatise written to convince a
heathen friend of the paramount claims of Christianity. He founds largely on the Old Testament,
but he also refers to the New, and quotes Timothy
explicitly as 'the divine word' and John's Gospel
by name. He is also said to have written a
Harmony, and is known to have quoted the
Apocalypse.[1] His words regarding John are:
'The Holy Scriptures teach us, and all those who
are vessels of the Spirit, of whom is John, saying,
" In the beginning was the Word,"' etc. He is not
here making any distinction between the Old Testament as Scripture and the New Testament as inspired; but in conformity with his principles, setting
all on the same level as vessels of the Spirit, or men
borne on by the Spirit, πνευματοφόροι or πνευματό-
φοροι (Reuss). With the quotations of Theophilus
we may be supposed to have come out of the thicket
to beaten tracks, for Irenæus was publishing his
great work on Heresies at the same time as Theo-

---

[1] See *Canonicity*, pp. 73, 182. See the opinions of Theophilus on the Inspiration of Scripture in *Ad Autol.* ii. 22, 33, 35; also iii. 12, 14.

philus wrote to his heathen friend ;[1] and in Irenæus' systematic treatise we find that our New Testament is the Canon, inspired, authoritative, and long closed. The history of the Canon ceases to be matter of dispute when we enter with Irenæus on the last quarter of the second century, although there is still some skirmishing over the claim of one or two individual books to be in the sacred list.

But we may be asked whether we have no authorities save those chance quotations of individual writers. And we have to answer that no systematic treatise on Christian doctrine has come down to us from an earlier date than that of Irenæus, though with him the great series begins to which the works of his younger contemporaries, Tertullian and Clement of Alexandria, and after them of Origen, belong. But we are not without tidings of the views of the collective Church at this same time. We have versions, or translations of the New Testament, rendering the original into the Latin and Syrian languages. Those versions date from the second century. One is at first surprised that Paul should write to the 'Romans' in Greek, not in Latin, and that a Latin translation of the Gospels was not forthcoming almost as soon as the originals were written. But Greek was on an equality with Latin as the tongue of the Roman Empire at and after the Christian era.

---

[1] Irenæus wrote Books I. and II. not later than A.D. 182.

In the Roman Senate, in domestic intercourse, in the commercial transactions in the seaports of the Mediterranean, and even in Palestine itself, men spoke their thoughts in Greek. An early Syriac tradition has it that Mark's Gospel was written in Latin and at Rome,[1] and though this is more than probable, the Latin original, if it existed, was soon lost ; and it is usually supposed that for the first hundred years from the time of the apostles the New Testament existed only in Greek. Enthusiastic scholars have even made it appear that our Lord spake in Greek in the highlands of Judea and in the fishing villages of Galilee. But though this is probably far-fetched, the mob of Jerusalem expected to be addressed in Greek when a tumult had brought them together (Acts xxii. 2), and were surprised into greater silence when the language was Hebrew. If Greek were thus current even in Palestine, we can understand what it must have been in Asia and Italy.

It was not for Rome, therefore, but for Africa that the first Latin New Testament was needed. All along the northern coast of Africa was a large Latin-speaking native community, associated with the Roman colonists, and for them at an early date translations of books of the New Testament were needed and were made. They were probably at first separate, and circulating in various forms, but

---

[1] See Moesinger's *Ephrem Syrus*, p. 286.

eventually some of them were collected so as to
furnish a Latin Testament, to which authority was
ascribed. This version had been current long
before the end of the century, long enough to
mould popular speech and to be itself revised;
and whether made in Africa itself or in Italy, or
whether made in Africa and revised in Italy, its
rude, strong rendering made it the people's Bible
of the great African Church. What, then, did
this Christian Bible contain? In Tertullian's
time, before the end of the century, it contained all
our New Testament save Second Peter, though
Hebrews does not seem to have been in it at first,
and James is not in all the copies.

In like manner a translation was made for the
Syrian Church. It was in Syria that the Christians
first received their name, because there they first
took shape as an organized body distinct from the
Jews. Early traditions tell of an Eastern Syrian
king, who wrote asking Jesus Christ to leave the
inhospitable and unbelieving Jews, and promising
Him shelter and favour in his own more kindly
realm; and they also tell that our Lord, who
would not leave the coasts of Israel, promised to
send an apostle. They further tell of apostles
going when the Lord had risen and finding a
willing people in Eastern Syria. This shows, at
least, how early Syria became leavened with
Christianity. We do not know when the Syriac

translation was made : early statements ascribe it
to the apostolic age, but whether this be so or not,
we cannot fix the date of the Syriac version of the
New Testament later than early in the second
century.   Hegesippus quoted 'from the Syriac'
(Euseb. *II. E.*, iv. 22).   Our remains of Greek
Christian literature are scanty enough ; of Syriac
directly we have none from that early date ; but
there is reason to believe that a Syriac New
Testament was in existence long before we can
find an explicit quotation of it.   So far as we
know, it wanted from the first, as it still wants,
the Apocalypse, Jude, Second Peter, and Second
and Third John.

There is one strange document, found in Milan
a hundred years ago, and named after its finder
Muratori, an eminent antiquary, 'The Muratorian
Fragment.'   Whether it was a formal document
compiled by men acting in concert, or whether it
was a letter from one man to another, nobody can
tell, for it has neither beginning nor end.   When
found it seemed to be part of some one's common-
place book, for there were other fragments beside
it.   Its barbarous Latin and peculiar phrases lead
to the opinion that it is probably a translation from
the Greek ; and from his speaking of the times of
Pius, Bishop of Rome, as being 'very lately in our
own times,' the original author must have written
soon after the middle of the second century.

It is the earliest attempt in existence to state
in detail what books the collection of Christian
Scriptures contains. Even, however, if we admit
this strange document to be of the early date
which it claims, and if we get over all the difficulty
of regarding an unauthenticated fragment as an
infallible authority, there is still no little doubt as
to its testimony on some points. It is so obscure
that in one or two places almost anything may be
made of it. It speaks of some books which are
otherwise unknown—as when it talks of an Epistle
to the Alexandrians, and of a Book of Wisdom,
written in honour of Solomon by his friends.[1] It
seems to tell of works of men who have not been
heard of in the field of Christian authorship, as
Miltiades[2] and Arsinous. But córruption of the
text may account for most of those inexplicable
passages, and its early date is made more probable
when we see on its list a few other books standing
apparently alongside of those usually accepted.

Having put those minute points aside, and check-
ing the desire to speculate upon their enigmas, we
find that the broad outlines which remain are most
interesting. Though the beginning is lost, so that
Matthew and Mark are not named, there can be no

---

[1] There is a happy conjecture that Φίλων was really the name of Philo,
to whom the authorship was ascribed, and that the translator mistook
it for 'friends.'

[2] Criticism overleaps itself in the attempt to make this word into
Tatian! But the attempt has been made.

doubt that they were on the list which now begins at Luke, and in which John is said to be the fourth. It testifies to the Acts of the Apostles, to thirteen Epistles of Paul, to two, or perhaps three, Epistles of John, to the Epistle of Jude, and to the Apocalypse of John. There is no certain mention of Hebrews; and (if the text be not corrupt) there is distinct mention of the Apocalypse of Peter, though Peter's Epistles, like James', are not named. John's Gospel is said to have been written at the request of his fellow-disciples, and after they had fasted together. All the Gospels are said to come from one primary Spirit, and therefore to maintain and manifest the unity of the faith.

There is much controversy about the principle on which the unknown author made up his Canon, or at least believed the Church to have made it up. By the simple process of reading into it all which he wishes to take out, an eminent living critic [1] proves a great many wonderful things from this Muratorian Fragment. Thus he proves that the author admitted only what was at once apostolical and ecclesiastically catholic, so that Paul's Epistles were admitted because he wrote to seven churches, as John wrote in the Apocalypse —seven being the perfect catholic number. But the distinguished critic has no ground for this idea of ecclesiastically catholic. The Epistles of

---

[1] Harnack, in *Brieger's Zeitschrift* for 1879, p. 358 ff.

Paul may make up a catholic number, but no one of them (unless it be Ephesians) was written to more than one church. The author of the Fragment distinctly says that the Epistles of Paul show the reason, the special occasion, and the particular place for which they were written. There is nothing about catholicity in that. Nor, as a matter of fact, were the 'Catholic Epistles,' as we have them in the New Testament, the first to find acceptance. The Epistles of James and Peter and Hebrews are not recognised by this very author, though their addresses are more catholic than most of those he does recognise. Again, the critic has to invent a new principle when accounting for the reception into the collection of Paul's letters to Timothy, Titus, and Philemon. It is the catholicity of their contents, their influence in establishing ecclesiastical discipline (which is explained to mean all 'the functions of the Christian Church, *except such as are doctrinal*').[1] But the Epistles to Timothy and Titus are as full of doctrine as of practice— of doctrine, too, put forward with a sharp point and a double edge. And, moreover, while one may speak of those letters as establishing church discipline, who can say the same of Philemon? That beautiful, personal, social, domestic Epistle

---

[1] *Alle christlich-kirchlichen Functionen mit Ausnahme der dogmatischen*, p. 586.

does not make the return of Onesimus have
anything to do with any discipline but that of
the law of love. No stronger proof can be found
of the straits to which one is put who adjusts
his facts to his theory instead of his theory
to the facts, than the further statement of this
eminent critic, that while Paul's letters were read,
Paul himself was forgotten. As if any man
could read Corinthians and Galatians and forget
Paul!

The author of the Muratorian Fragment had
much simpler principles than the Giessen critic.
He knew that there is a Spirit pervading the
Church, and forming its faith ; and that those
books are at one with that faith, and come from
that one Spirit. He accepts none that have not
apostolic origin, save those which, like Luke, have
apostolic sanction. Paul's Epistles were written
to particular churches for particular needs, but the
Spirit moved him as He moved John to write to
seven churches and no more. Paul's letters to
individuals were written from affection and love,
but they are hallowed by the whole Church,
because of the rules of instruction which they
lay down. I do not think that he rests the
acceptance of the books upon the opinion of the
Church ; it is better to say that he rests it on
the harmony of the Spirit which is in them with
the Spirit and the faith of the Church. But he

is quite clear that a book written like Hermas in the middle of the second century is—just because that was its date—never to the end of time to be read in the Church, nor counted with ·the prophets, whose number is complete, nor with the apostles. And the work of the heretics, Marcion and the rest, he scouts.

This old document always seems to be older the more closely we study it; and it is with fresh conviction of its age after renewed study that I point to those principles of the author, as showing how men thought about the New Testament in the middle of the second century.

At the close of the second century there are three men standing out from all the rest; one (*Irenæus*) a bishop in Lyons, and two African presbyters—*Clement* in Alexandria, and *Tertullian* in Carthage. *Irenæus* comes first. He was a native of Asia Minor, a pupil of Polycarp, who was (as we have seen) the pupil of the Apostle John. He went from Asia to Gaul, and was chosen bishop of Lyons in A.D. 178. He had been before that sent from Gaul to Rome as a deputy of the Gallic Church; and thus, on at least one occasion, became personally acquainted with those who 'seemed to be pillars of the Church' in the metropolis, and with the leading heretics also. He was so impressed with the peril to which false teachers were bringing the members of the

Church, especially those without clear brains,[1] that after meeting the heretics and reading their books, he devoted himself on his return to Gaul to composing an elaborate account and Refutation of all Heresies. In this learned, fair, and cautious book, Irenæus habitually quotes the passages of Scripture on which heretics relied, and those also which, in his opinion, they contravened. From those erudite and careful quotations we find that Irenæus founded upon the four Gospels, the Acts, twelve Epistles of Paul (Philemon is not named, and Hebrews is not acknowledged), the First of Peter, and the First and Second of John, and the Apocalypse. He founded upon them as upon an immovable rock. There are for him no books like the Bible-books, and the New Testament is Bible to him beyond all question. He repeatedly calls it γραφαί—'Scriptures;' and he speaks of the New Testament as falling into two divisions, — 'Evangelic and Apostolic,' — a division dating from Marcion, which we find Clement of Alexandria and Origen adopting with the names 'The Gospel' and 'The Apostle.'[2] He is one of many to say that Mark wrote his Gospel as the contents of the preaching of Peter, whose 'scholar and interpreter' Mark was; and he is, so far as we know, the first to say that Luke wrote his Gospel as what Paul preached. His

---

[1] ἐπεὶ μὴ πάντες τὸν ἐγκέφαλον ἐξεπτύκασι, he says, as showing why some are not heretics. See *Ref. Hær.* Pref. § 2.

[2] See many references, *Canonicity*, pp. 45, 46.

well - known words may be quoted here : 'Since there are four climes of the world in which we live, and four great winds, and since the Church has been spread over all the world, and since the gospel and the Spirit of Life is the pillar and strength of the Church, it is fitting that it [the gospel] has four Pillars breathing out imperishable truth on every side, and kindling life in men. Whence it is evident that the Logos (Word), who is Maker of all, who sitteth upon the cherubim, and controlleth all, when He had been manifested to men, gave to us a gospel under four aspects, but bound together by one Spirit.   There were also four general covenants given to humanity ; the first that of Noah's deluge, with the sign of the bow ; the second, Abraham's, with the sign of circumcision ; the third, the giving of law under Moses ; and the fourth, that of the gospel through our Lord Jesus Christ.' [1]

Contemporary with him, but about twenty years later in birth and death, was *Tertullian*, the fiery advocate of Carthage.   In his later life he adopted the heresy of Montanism, — the Irvingism of the second century, — but through life he was the eloquent and impassioned defender of Christianity against Jews, heretics, and heathen.   His habit was to establish his point by a series of systematic

---

[1] Iren. *Hær.* iii. 11, 8. *Canonicity*, pp. 68, 69. See note on ' Irenæus ' at the end of Lecture vi.

quotations taken from the books of the New Testament in their order; so that, when he does not name a book or a text which would bear on his point, we may infer that he did not know it or did not accept it. He uses all our New Testament except James, Second Peter, and Second and Third John; but it is clear that Hebrews was not part of the Canon of the African Church which he represented. The eloquent words in which he descants upon the wide spread of Christianity through the Roman Empire have been already quoted.[1]

Irenæus was a man of many lands, and his writings, though originally in Greek, come to us in an old Latin translation, save the passages which have been quoted by later writers; Tertullian is a Latin writer, quoting the old Latin New Testament of which we have spoken; but the next we have to name is a Greek philosopher, teacher, and Christian. *Clement of Alexandria* has one of the noblest names in Christian history. Full of learning, generous by disposition, representing fully the eclectic tendencies of the great commercial city in which he lived and laboured, he is an admirable type of a devout and learned Christian. He is so generous in his estimate of the good that lurks in many things alien from his own position, that we find him not only trying

---

[1] See before, p. 51.

to show what good there is in a true Gnosis—
a Gnosis (knowledge, as he explains) which is
drawn from the truth proved by the Scriptures
themselves, but we find him also ascribing
prophetic inspiration to the strange Sibylline
oracles ; commenting on Barnabas and the
Apocalypse of Peter ; and quoting freely (but
by way of illustration) from many apocryphal
books. But although his generous mind and his
training as an eclectic, and a literary man of
wide reading, made Clement thus admit the claims
on his attention made by all those books, it does
not appear that he set any of them—not even
the Sibyl—on the platform of Holy Scripture.
And the books of our New Testament were his
New Testament Scripture, save that we find no
mention of James, Second Peter, and Third John.
His principle was that, while all Christians have
the gift and grace of God's Holy Spirit, the
apostles had the Spirit in complete measure ;[1] so
that his Rule of Faith is found in the agreement
of the Church, and the apostles, and the prophets.
In the case of Clement, we have first to distinguish
the literary man from the theologian, and then,
even in estimating the testimony of the theologian
to our Scriptures, we have to remember that he
did not write with a critical but with a practical
object in view.

[1] See footnote, p. 94.

The third century of our era has some great names, as Hippolytus, Caius, Dionysius, Cyprian, but none so great as the name of Origen, who followed Clement as head of the catechetical school of Alexandria.   By this time Christendom had come to practical agreement upon the new volume of the Scriptures; and while some books were only accepted in some places, more than twenty of them were universally acknowledged.   But Origen introduced biblical criticism, strictly so called, into the field.   He dealt with the Greek versions of the Old Testament in a thoroughly critical way, arranging all of them in parallel columns, so that the Septuagint and its rivals (the versions of Aquila, Symmachus, and Theodotion) might be easily compared at a glance.   What he arranged was, moreover, a critical text; and his marks and symbols, designed to show the value of particular readings, are still intelligible as a proof of the thoroughness and patience of the great critic of the third century.   This invaluable work was lost,[1] and the same fate has befallen most of the five thousand volumes of notes, commentaries, and homilies which the indefatigable scholar wrote.   He 'wrote more

---

[1] It was preserved in the library at Cæsarea. Jerome saw it there. It was there in the sixth century, but it perished with the library in some siege. What remains are transcripts of the principal readings in the column containing the Septuagint—transcripts originally suggested, and enriched with marginal notes, by Eusebius and Pamphilus. See Dr. Field's Prolegomena to his splendid edition, especially pp. xcix.-ci.

than any other man can read,' says the next
greatest critic in Christian history. The glimpse
we have into his work in a passage of Eusebius'
Church History (vi. 23) gives an idea of his enor-
mous labour. 'He had more than seven shorthand
writers to whom he dictated, who relieved each
other at appointed times; he had as many book-
writers, and along with them girls, skilled in
beautiful penmanship.' For all this staff Origen
himself had no means of providing, but the inex-
pressible zeal of his friend Ambrosius supplied it
all abundantly, and gratitude to Ambrosius stimu-
lated the superhuman toil of the patient scholar
who calls his rich friend his taskmaster.[1] At an
early period of his life Origen gave up his own
patrimony and sold his library that he might be
without care for the things of this world; but care
pursues the footsore pedestrian as well as the
mounted man, and Origen's life was one of priva-
tion, was indeed in the end worn out by destitution
and trouble after the death of Ambrosius. This is
not the place to tell the romantic story of his
devoted life; but the troubles he brought upon
himself that he might be a true disciple of Jesus,
are the guarantee of his single-mindedness and
truthfulness, with which we are much concerned.

When we try to sum up the opinions of this
great scholar, we find from his extant Greek

---

[1] ἐργοδιώκτης, Origen in Johan. T. v.

works, and Eusebius' extracts, that he accepted as
Scripture the four Gospels, the Acts of the
Apostles, thirteen Epistles of Paul, the Epistle to
the Hebrews, whether Paul's or not, First Peter,
First John, and the Apocalypse.　He mentions
Second Peter, and Second and Third John, but says
that they are of disputed genuineness.　In the
Latin translation of his Homilies we see that he
speaks of Second Peter and 'the Epistles' of John
as parts of the New Testament; and that he gives
the same rank to James and Jude.　In one place
he speaks of James and Jude as servants of God
digging wells of salvation; in another he speaks
of James and Jude and Peter (in two Epistles) as
sounding the gospel trumpets under the new and
greater Joshua, of whose conquering hosts they are
the priests, whose blasts bring down the Jericho of
heathenism and false philosophy.[1]

Eusebius,[2] who knew the worth of Origen's
testimony, says :

'In the first book of his Commentaries on Matthew, observing
the ecclesiastical Canon, he testifies that he knows only four
Gospels, saying thus : What I have learned from tradition regarding the four Gospels, which alone have no word said against
them in the Church of God, which is under heaven, is to the effect
that the first written was that according to Matthew, once a
publican, afterwards an apostle of Jesus Christ, and that he
published it for Jews which believed, and that it was written in
the Hebrew tongue; the second was that according to Mark, who

---

[1] See *Homilies* on Gen. xiii. 2; Josh. vii. 2; *Canonicity*, pp. 51, 52.
[2] Euseb. *H. E.* vi. 25; *Canonicity*, p. 8.

made it according to Peter's recital, and of whom Peter speaks as
his son in his Catholic Epistle, saying, "The elect lady which is
in Babylon salutes you, as also does Marcus my son;" the third
was the Gospel commended by St. Paul, viz. that according to
Luke, who wrote for Gentile converts; and last of all, the Gospel
according to John.'

Origen here not only testifies to the apostolic
sanction given to the Gospels of Mark and Luke,
but he seems to speak of the Gospels as composed
in the order in which they now stand.

On the Epistles he says : 'Paul, who was fitted to be the minister
of the new covenant, not of the letter but of the spirit, who fulfilled
the gospel from Jerusalem and round about unto Illyricum, did
not write unto all the churches which he taught, and sent only a
few lines to those to which he did write. And Peter, on whom
is built the Church of Christ, against which the gates of Hades
shall not prevail, has left one Epistle acknowledged to be his.
Let there be reckoned also a Second, but it is disputed. What
shall I say of him who laid back his head upon the breast of
Jesus, who has left one Gospel, avowing that he could write so
many that the world should not be able to contain them? He
wrote the Apocalypse also, having been ordered to keep silence
and not to write the voices of the seven thunders. He has left
also an Epistle of very few lines. Let there be reckoned also a
Second and a Third, since all do not admit them to be genuine.
But both of them do not contain more than a hundred lines.'

We may conclude our historical survey with a
quotation from the man to whom more than to any
other, or, indeed, than to all others put together,
we owe our knowledge of the first three hundred
years of Christian history. Eusebius was born
about A.D. 260, and died, full of years and honours,
after a life of great industry, in A.D. 339. He was
the friend and trusted counsellor of Constantine

the Great; to him we probably owe the Sinaitic
MS. recently discovered, as it seems to have been
one of the fifty he was directed by his imperial
friend to prepare for the use of the churches in
Constantinople; and to him above all we owe
(among many other works) the History of the
Church from the earliest days to his own, in which
all the writings of all the worthies are described,
and in which as quotation or description we find all
we know of some of the most important products
of Christian thought.   It was his custom to collect
with special care whatever any one had said about
the disputed books of the New Testament, and
about such extra - canonical books as those of
Barnabas and Clement, which bulked most largely
in the estimation of Christians.   He did not concern himself with the ancient testimonies to books
which no one disputed.   This 'silence of Eusebius'
has been often misunderstood, as though some
ancient worthy did not use a book—say a gospel—
when Eusebius does not say that he did; but the
foremost English scholar of our day has made it for
ever clear that Eusebius of set purpose did not en-
cumber his narrative with superfluous testimonies
to books, the canonical place and authority [1] of
which nobody disputed.   Eusebius says [2] :—

---

[1] Bishop Lightfoot on 'The Silence of Eusebius,' *Contemporary
Review* (1875, p. 169).
[2] *H. E.* iii. 25; see the text, with notes, in *Canonicity*, p. 10.

'Having come thus far it is proper to sum up the testimonies which have been adduced to the Scriptures of the New Testament. First of all, then, must be placed the holy quartette of the Gospels, which are followed by the writing of the Acts of the Apostles. After it are to be ranked the Epistles of Paul, followed in due order by the First Epistle circulated under John's name, and likewise also is to be approved the Epistle of Peter. Next to those are to be arranged, if you see good, the Apocalypse of John, my opinions concerning which we shall set forth in due time. These, then, are to be set down as *accepted* (Homologoumena). Further, to the class of writings *disputed*, but familiar to the majority of people, belong the Epistle circulated in the name of James, and that of Jude, and the Second of Peter, and the Second and Third with the name of John, whether they really belong to the Evangelist or to another John. As a class of *spurious* books, let there be reckoned the writing of the Acts of Paul, and that which is called The Shepherd (Hermas), and the Apocalypse of Peter, and with them the book current as the Epistle of Barnabas, and the so-called Doctrines of the Apostles; and also, as I said before, the Apocalypse of John, if you think fit ; for this is a writing which, as I said, some reject but others adjudge to the class of *accepted* books. There are likewise some who have referred to this class the Gospel according to the Hebrews, in which those Hebrews who have accepted Christ take special delight. All of those may perhaps be counted among disputed books. It is from necessity that we have made a detailed catalogue of such books, distinguishing those which, according to ecclesiastical tradition, are true and unforged, and fully accepted, from those others alongside of them which are not in the covenant, but are disputed, and yet known by most people of the Church, so that we may have good grounds for knowing those others also which, being put forward by heretics under the names of apostles, as though they were Gospels of Peter and Thomas and Matthias, or as containing acts of some of the rest,—of Andrew, for example, or of John, and of the other apostles,—nothing of which has been ever thought worth mentioning in his writings by a single man in the succession of ecclesiastics. Moreover, the style of expression (in them) is somehow quite different from the apostolic usage, and the thought and plan of the things brought forward in them, as alien as it is possible to be from true orthodoxy, clearly betoken that we are dealing with the fabrications of heretical men. Wherefore let such writings be not put down even among the spurious, but let them be cast aside as altogether *worthless* and *impious.*'

The opinions of his age are collected by Eusebius in this passage, and from it we see that the greatest part of the New Testament was accepted without dispute throughout Christendom. We see that there were other books accepted by most, but not with the same heartiness by all; and the notes we have made on earlier lists have prepared us to learn what those books were. They are James and Jude, Second Peter, and Second and Third John. Some add the Apocalypse of John. All these books, save James, were wanting in the New Testament of the Syriac Church, which, being the earliest collection of Christian Scripture for the East, had great influence on the views of all the Oriental Churches, for which Eusebius was specially qualified to speak. When we turn to the Western or Latin Church, we find that *James* was probably omitted in the old Italic collection current in Africa, and that Second Peter certainly was. What Eusebius, therefore, tells us with his usual candid truthfulness is what we should have known from those other sources; and it may be regarded as established beyond dispute.

Let us now inquire whether there be anything in those books already named as among the Anti-

legomena of Eusebius which accounts for their lack
of universal recognition. It need not surprise us
that the two short letters of *John* were omitted
in many collections. They are short, they are
personal ; and except that they were believed to
come from the Great Apostle, they would not have
bulked largely in the estimation of the Church.
The Epistle of *James* is in another position. It
was accepted in the Eastern Church from the first.
It is not found in the Muratorian Canon, or in the
majority of the MSS. of the old Latin. Irenæus'
quotations may be drawn from Paul, not from
James. Not until the beginning of the third
century gives us the testimony of Hippolytus (an
Italian bishop), are we sure of its being in the
Bible of the Latin Church. James wrote to the
Jews of the dispersion ; and as they were found in
the East rather than in the West (he himself never
left Jerusalem), the first circulation and the chief
popularity of this letter were in the East. The
Jews were not so numerous in the cities of
Europe (Rome excepted), and this Epistle was
not therefore so important in the western regions
of the Church. Those European churches, too,
were essentially Pauline ; and the doctrine of
James, who was not personally known as Paul
and Peter were in the West, has always at first
sight been a difficulty to those whose faith is
sustained from the truth as Paul teaches it. Thus

we can see how the Epistle was slow in winning its place ; and we infer that overwhelming evidence of its genuineness must have been on its side, or it would never have overcome the barriers in its way.

The cases of *Second Peter* and *Jude* are so similar as to require being considered together. It is not possible to resist the conviction that the author of the one Epistle took some verses from the other ; and as Jude is the more distinct and explicit, it seems on the whole probable that his Epistle was the earlier. Both seem to have been written to Jews, and before the fall of Jerusalem ; for both are full of Hebrew memories, and in neither is there any allusion to the ruin of the Holy City. Paul was still living when Peter wrote. Apostles had personally spoken to those whom Jude addressed. Both those Epistles seem to have drifted away into nooks and corners among the Jewish Christian people, and it was long ere either of them had universal recognition. Yet they were known to many. Tertullian calls Jude an apostle, though he himself does not claim that honoured rank. Origen also does so. Clement of Alexandria commented on the Second Epistle of Peter, and Irenæus, and even Justin Martyr, used it. There is thus early testimony in favour of both letters. On the whole, although of all the books of our New Testament Canon those two Epistles are

least supported by external testimony, and although
their obscurity has militated against their reception,
they were eventually accepted by the Church of
Christ, because they were believed to come . from
apostles. The date at which they appeared was
before Gnosticism had much hold of the Jewish
Christian, but after lawlessness — Antinomianism
in personal life—was prevalent.

The history of the acceptance of the *Apocalypse*
is unlike that which belongs to any other book.
It has had vicissitudes ; it has been the most
popular and the most unpopular of books, and this
too by turns, for it has been more than once at
each extreme. The early Church, expecting an
immediate return of the Lord, believed that it
found an announcement of the fact in the Apocalypse, though it seems to us strange that such an
idea could prevail, or that all the woes and experiences could be supposed to be crowded into a few
years. Papias quoted the book with no misgivings,
and Justin Martyr quotes it by name, though he
does not so quote any other book of the New
Testament. We read that in a work now lost he
expounded it ; and the same is true of Irenæus.
Origen and Hippolytus honoured it as coming from
the Apostle John, and up till that time (the third
century) it stood high everywhere,—alike in the
East and in the West,—save that, for some reason
which we do not understand, it is absent from

the Syriac New Testament. But in the third
century, as men began to despair of the speedy
coming of the King, they began also to disparage
the book on which many of the Millenarians had
professed to base their expectations. Papias had
given special umbrage by his grotesque illustrations and traditions on the subject of the personal
reign of Christ upon earth; and, in the recoil from
those exaggerations, prudent men went so far as to
deny that the Apostle John could have been the
authority to which (however falsely) the Millenarians betook themselves for their warrant. So
one eminent Roman presbyter (Caius) ascribed the
book, not to John, but to Cerinthus, John's great
adversary; and an Alexandrian scholar (Dionysius)
composed with great acumen an elaborate argument
to prove from the style that the apostle who
wrote the fourth Gospel could not have written the
Apocalypse. Eusebius, who was cold though candid,
had a great horror of Millenarianism, and loses no
opportunity of disparaging those who favoured the
Apocalypse, or of hinting that the book itself
might be thrown aside altogether. In the Eastern
Church Cyril of Jerusalem kept up this dubiety;
in the Western Church Jerome's authority caused
it to pass away, and brought the Apocalypse into
high esteem. At the Reformation the hints of
Erasmus were carried to all lengths by Luther and
Zwingli, who tossed the book away. Calvin was

more prudent, alike in the fact of his using the book and in that of not venturing to write a commentary upon it. Its want of definite doctrine, though its practical religious teaching is as clear as its predictions are obscure, caused those reformers to lay little stress upon a book which told nothing of justification by faith, that 'article of a standing or a falling church.' But in the next century, when it was not for doctrines but for church systems that men fought, when Bossuet saw in it the prediction of the sins of Protestantism, and Vitringa found the iniquities of Popery, both Protestants and Roman Catholics honoured the book with eager deference. In our own day it has the curious fate of being the most prized book in the scanty Canon of the Tübingen school, who see in it a weapon against the fourth Gospel, and of being looked at askance by many good Christians, who are repelled by the mystery of its many symbols. Other good Christians, on the other hand, find in its opening and closing chapters a richer feast of holy hope than anywhere else in the New Testament; and many who are burdened with the woes of the body of Christ in an unbelieving world, find—as did Ezekiel among the captive Hebrews — a strong consolation in the vision of the new Jerusalem, the holy city, which God will establish among men.

We see in this history how doctrinal views

have contributed to the favour or the dislike with which a book may be regarded.

There is another book of the Canon, from studying the history of which we may learn a different lesson. The *Epistle to the Hebrews* has never from the very first been doubted in the Eastern Church; but it was three hundred years and more before it was generally accepted in the West, although it was in the Old Latin Canon before Tertullian's time. The cause of this acceptance in the East and lack of acceptance in the West is its being addressed to Alexandrian Jews, who regarded it as Paul's; while in other parts of the Church, to which it came somewhat later, the want of distinct proof of Pauline authorship caused its canonical position to be doubted. There was also against it in the orthodox West its apparent countenance (vi. 4, 8) to the views of the Montanists, who maintained that the lapsed should never be restored to church privileges.[1] But in the East it was believed to be Paul's, and as such was accepted. Some thought that Clement of Rome translated it from Paul's Hebrew,—some that Luke did this service for Paul,—but that it was Paul's they were sure. Of this Clement of Alexandria is undoubted proof. In the West the Muratorian Canon seems to refer to it as a forgery. Hippolytus and Irenæus

---

[1] This seems to have been Caius' reason. See *Canonicity*, p. 279, note.

deny that it was Paul's. Tertullian ascribed its composition to Barnabas ; but he at the same time takes care to say that Barnabas was a man sufficiently accredited of God. Thus in the West it was not universally accepted, because Paul was not recognised as the author ; while in the East, there being little or no doubt of the Pauline authorship,—though there were many guesses as to the translator or amanuensis,—there was no difficulty in accepting it. Origen undertakes to prove that it is Paul's, though elsewhere he admits that there are such peculiarities of style as to make him think that Clement or Luke may have been the actual penman of Paul's thoughts in it.

Thus we find a principle that the proof of apostolic authorship led to acceptance of a book as authoritative. But this we must reserve for next lecture.

NOTE ON THE DISCOVERY OF TATIAN'S
'DIATESSARON.'

In the second volume of the Armenian edition of the works of
Ephrem Syrus, is a book inscribed, 'An Exposition of the Con-
cordant Gospel made by S. Ephrem, Syrian Doctor.' The
Armenian text dates from A.D. 1195 (there are two MSS. of it),
and is a very literal translation from the Syriac—so literal, indeed,
that many Syriac constructions remain in the Armenian. This
was rendered into very literal Latin by Father Aucher in 1841,
and revised and compared with the original Armenian MS. by
Professor Moesinger of Salzburg, in 1876. The interest which
attaches to this ancient document arises from its possibly being
a translation of a Commentary by Ephrem Syrus on the *Diatessaron*
of Tatian. That Tatian wrote a book which was a blending of
the four Gospels, may be regarded as amply established. There
is Syrian testimony establishing the fact of Ephrem expounding
or explaining Tatian's work. The questions, therefore, are—(1)
Can the commentary or exposition thus recovered through the
Armenian be rightly ascribed to Ephrem? (2) Can the work
commented on be identified with Tatian's Harmony?

The answer to (1) the first question is partly founded on many
minute points, which, when viewed together, furnish a cogent
argument. Even in the Armenian the style is like that of Ephrem;
the mode of commenting is the same as that which he follows when
dealing with the Old Testament, *i.e.* the notes are usually terse
and helpful, attached to obscure or difficult expressions, but
sometimes (as, *e.g.*, in regard to the birth of John Baptist, or the
woman with the issue of blood) they are disproportionately diffuse;
the references to contemporary events (as when the expositor, in a
prayer appended to the Exposition, speaks of his Church being
robbed of its pastor) agree with what is known of Ephrem's time;
the incessant and vigorous thrusts at the Marcionites are charac-
teristic of Ephrem; and some peculiar views of his regarding Old
Testament incidents appear from time to time in this Commentary.
There are other considerations which it needs no expert to judge.
Dionysius Barsalibi (a Mesopotamian, A.D. 1171) says that

Tatian's Harmony began with the words (from John's Gospel), '*In the beginning was the Word.*' This we find to be the case in the text of the Commentary before us. It is said to have been a unification of the Gospels; it was not a Harmony in the sense of a comparison or collocation of passages; and we find that our text passes from the opening words of John's Gospel (John i. 1, 5, but vers. 10, 14, 17 are also quoted) to Luke i. 5 : ' There was in the days of Herod the king,' etc., giving an account of the nativity of the Baptist. After notes on the leading verses of Luke i., the Exposition proceeds to remark upon the betrothal of Joseph and Mary, in Matt. i. 18, 25. Then follow the Magi, the mission of the Jews to John (John i. 19–28), etc. And so the expositor goes on ; evidently with a text before him which is woven together from the four Gospels, and on what seem to him the salient points of it he makes remarks sometimes critical, sometimes practical. On the whole, the Exposition does not seem to have been designed for a congregation, but it quite suggests the idea of its being notes of lectures to students of theology. There was a theological school in Edessa to the pupils in which Ephrem may have addressed his remarks. The occasional references to 'the Greek' are intelligible when this is kept in mind. Ephrem was not usually a preacher ; he was only in deacon's orders; but he was a teacher and a theologian. On the whole, everything points to this being the work of the great Syrian father, to whom an unswerving tradition ascribes the composition of such a work.

(2) The second question—on the identification of the work with Tatian's Harmony—also admits of an affirmative answer. First of all, there is no mention of any other work of the same kind in antiquity. The Harmony of Ammonius was quite different, being merely the Gospel of Matthew, with the parallel paragraphs from the other Gospels placed alongside, or indicated by an ingenious system of descriptive marks, as explained by Eusebius in his letter to Carpian. Tatian's work was not such a collocation ; it was the ' making of one from four ;' and what Ephrem comments upon was such a unification of our four Gospels. As we have seen, Tatian's work began with John's prologue, and omitted the genealogies. So does this ; and the case appears to be made out. There is, however, one difficulty. Theodoret (about A.D. 450), who found 200 copies of Tatian's Harmony in his diocese, and believing them to be heretical, put them away, says that Tatian cut away the genealogies and all references in our Gospels to

Christ being of the seed of David according to the flesh. We find in the work on which Ephrem comments that the blind man of Jericho and the children of Jerusalem do call upon the Son of David. This makes a difficulty which it is impossible to overlook. But (1) Theodoret probably saw that at the outset there is an omission in Matt. i. 20, of 'Joseph the son of David,' and a curious silence about Bethlehem (David's city) as the place of enrolment, and hastily assumed that the other references to the Saviour's descent from David were also omitted. It is true that almost at the outset (Moesinger, p. 16) the commentator remarks: 'The same Scripture says in another place that both Joseph and Mary were of the house of David,' but it is not at all certain that he found this in the Harmony. He seems to have been using his own knowledge of the Gospels in their simple form. (2) Theodoret probably did not read the whole book carefully. What he saw on the first page was enough to satisfy him that the Harmony was dangerously imperfect; and he may have rashly announced that the whole work was like its first pages. And (3) the passages where the blind man and the multitude call upon Jesus as David's son may have seemed to Theodoret to indicate the opinion of the multitude only; while what he desiderated was the testimony of the Evangelists (as in the genealogies) to our Lord's Davidic descent. That Theodoret thus judged is rendered probable by the fact that Marcion sometimes distinguished in this way between the statement of the Evangelist and that of the people. For example, he omitted Luke viii. 19, and retained v. 20.

On the whole, while not concealing that there is some difficulty in disposing of the words of Theodoret, the book now in our hands may be accepted as the long-lost Commentary of Ephrem on the Harmony of Tatian.[1] It appears, moreover, that Tatian wrote his Harmony in his old age, when he had left Rome after dwelling there for many years, and that he wrote it in Syriac. It was not originally a Greek book; and as its circulation was mainly in the eastern regions of the Church, its existence became merely a rumour to ecclesiastics who dwelt in Rome or in Constantinople. But until the fourth, or even the fifth, century it was a popular

---

[1] The *Codex Fuldensis*, which we owe to Victor of Capua, seems to be Tatian's Harmony considerably altered. Luke's preface is put at the beginning, and immediately after comes John's prologue. The codex as a whole rests upon Tatian's Harmony, but many changes are made to adapt the text to Jerome's version.

book in Edessa and eastward. That 200 copies of it were found in one diocese amply proves this. Zahn has made it probable that Tatian (born A.D. 110 ; lived in Rome A.D. 155–173) returned to his native Mesopotamia when about sixty years of age, and then wrote this book, which made him dear to the Syrian Church.

The student may be referred to Aucher—Moesinger's *Evangelii Concordantis Expositio facta a S. Ephræmo doctore Syro* (Venetiis, 1876). No description is so easily understood as the work itself. With it may be compared Ranke's edition of the *Codex Fuldensis* (Marburg and Leipzig, 1868). The whole subject is exhaustively discussed in all its aspects in Zahn's *Forschungen zur Geschichte des N. T. Kanons*, 1 Theil., *Tatian's Diatessaron*, 1881. The articles of Harnack in Brieger's *Zeitschrift für Kirchengeschichte*, February 1881, are incisive and suggestive. They may be said to have awakened the attention of students to the importance of the discovery, though Moesinger, in his own modest preface, makes his opinion very clear. English readers will find excellent articles by Professor Wace in the *Expositor* for 1881 and 1882.

LECTURE VI.

BEFORE we proceed to the conclusion of our short
course, we must here look back on the principles
which guided Christendom to the conclusions at
which it arrived. There is not time for an
adequate examination, but we may indicate what
it is not possible on this occasion to illustrate
or even to expound.

The first utterances on the subject of our New
Testament books speak from the consciousness of
membership of a living Church, which had Christ
for its author and head. Clement of Rome (A.D. 90)
is expressing the mind of all when he says, as a
summary of all duty : 'Especially being mindful
of the words of the Lord Jesus which He spake'
(1 Clem. chap. xiii.). Again he says, when he
wishes to make men strong and trustful : 'For
God liveth, and the Lord Jesus Christ liveth, and
the Holy Spirit' (1 Clem. chap. lviii. 2). So
Polycarp (A.D. 155 or A.D. 166): 'Remembering
those things which the Lord said in His teaching:

Judge not, that ye be not judged,' etc.   If
the early Christians spoke of the apostles, it
was as witnesses after the Master, and to Him.
' Paul was a herald, and gained the fitting
(γενναῖον) renown of his faith' (Clem. chap. v.).
Peter was a ' witness' unto death.   On that
ground, those men, and the other apostles in
their measure, were reverenced as the messengers
of Christ.   It was because they had a message
from Christ, and the witness of the Holy Spirit
to it, that they were authoritative guides of the
Church.   The words of the Lord Jesus, and His
thoughts, and His work were the ultimate objects
of faith and striving.   Not so much the Gospels,
as the truths the Gospels contain, were the burden
of the speech and reasoning of those ' Ep. -
Apostolic' Christian teachers.

When it came to other writings than the Gospels,
and other words than those of the Master Himself,
the value attached by the Christian believers to
those writings sprang from the conviction that
their authors were commissioned to represent
Christ.   Thus Polycarp, as we have seen, says :
' For neither I, nor any other such, can come up
to the wisdom of the blessed and glorified Paul.
He, when among you, accurately and stedfastly
taught the word of truth.'   It was out of the
fulness of the Church's conscious life — of a life
consciously received in the word of Christ, and

of His commissioned apostles—that the believing membership drew the purpose of hallowing certain books as the vessels in which the treasure had come to them, and in which it might be found by others. Christendom was formed without a book. Christ formed it by making a personal tie with His first followers, and they extended it by bringing others into personal relationship with themselves, and through themselves with Him. There was a truth by which the people lived before its message was found in any book, but not before it was found on the lips of a man. Paul's preaching was known before Paul's letters were written. But when the letters appeared, it was because they were Paul's that they received welcome and deference. No other assurance than that a letter was his seemed to be necessary in any case. So 'weighty' were his letters, that a forged letter, 'as from him,' troubled the men of Thessalonica.

And thus the Canon of the New Testament was made up by men receiving and hallowing book after book as telling of Christ, and coming from His accredited messengers. The Gospels did not need an author's name in the same formal way as the Epistles, because the Gospels were esteemed for what they contained of Christ's words and deeds — the divine oracles, the λόγια from which the Church sprang. With those

words and deeds men were familiar, owing to the
much preaching of apostles and other eye-witnesses
and hearers of the word; and the written book
was valued in the measure of its containing the
familiar facts and sayings.   Accordingly, as
apostles taught orally everywhere the life and
work of Jesus Christ, there naturally arose in
many places short written accounts of the substance of that teaching, epitomes of the gospel,
more or less fragmentary, but serving a very
useful purpose for the time.   It was to such as
those St. Luke referred in his preface.   His
verdict on them is only that they were fragmentary and inadequate.   He claims for his own
that it is a complete digest of what they gave
partially.   His Gospel, therefore, and his Book
of the Acts, contain what is equivalent to an
avowal of his name, and an appeal to his
qualifications, which were well known to Theophilus and to the Church.   The other Gospels
contain no author's name, although it must have
been so well known at first as to prevent all
doubt or dispute.   The Evangelists were divinely
moved to do the work they did; but their own
personality did not need to be avowed.   They
were not teachers, like the writers of Epistles;
they were only reporters or annalists.   It was the
Lord who spake in His own Person.   The author's
name was no integral part of the composition;

men knew that the book was true because they recognised the truth of which it was full. But they knew also—the earliest testimonies show it —that while Matthew's Gospel and John's were by apostles, Mark's came with the authority of an epitome of Peter's preaching, and Luke's with a similar authority from Paul. 'Marcus, my son,' wrote as for Peter; 'Luke, the beloved physician,' who was with his great master in sorrow and trial unto the end, committed to writing a compendium of Christ's gospel such as Paul must have used; and thus, whether Paul formally authorized it or not, Luke's book was Paul's. We find that the early Church reasoned in this way, though we cannot here give details.

Then as to Epistles. They were accepted because they came from apostles. All Epistles were written to Christians. There is no trace of one written to Jews or to heathen; and what the Christians wanted to know about an Epistle was in brief whether it came from an apostle. There is no trace of any Epistle being accepted on any other ground than its apostolic authorship. Men had faith in the apostles. The 'signs of an apostle' had been wrought everywhere in the Church; and all Christians knew that apostles had authority to 'bind and loose.' That authority entitled them to write doctrinal and regulative treatises, which were statutes for the whole

Church of Christ. It was therefore a simple
question of authorship. The books about which
there was any question were books about which
there was uncertainty as to the author. Hebrews,
as we have seen, was for long a disputed book
in the Western Church, because men were not
satisfied that it came from Paul. It was accepted
as Paul's in Alexandria—to which city it was
sent—and over the East from the earliest times
downwards.[1] It was not so in the West.
Tertullian ascribes the Epistle to Barnabas; and
he quotes it in a significant way. He did not
think Barnabas an apostle in the sense of being
a founder of the Church; and though he described
that eminent Christian as a man 'sufficiently
accredited by God,' he regarded a quotation from
the Epistle to the Hebrews as 'redundant' rather
than relevant. And so far as one can see,
there was no controversy about the acceptance of
any Epistle, unless there were doubt about the
authorship.

It is not easy to state the case without apparently reasoning in a circle, or without ascribing
to something called the 'Collective Church' (a
thing which did not exist at all) the authority
to form a Canon. But still the fact is that the
miraculous constitution of the Christian society
which the Saviour came to establish, really led

---

[1] *Canonicity.* pp. 272, 280.

to the formation of this Canon, and is inseparable
from it.   Christ, the Supreme Life ; apostles, as
competent witnesses for Christ ; with those the
Church had come into living contact ; and Gospels
were received because they were true books about
Christ ; Epistles, because they came from the men
whom He had appointed to 'judge the twelve
tribes of Israel,' to 'bind and loose on earth
what would be bound and loosed in heaven.'
The Church was 'built upon the foundation of
the apostles and prophets, Jesus Christ Himself
being the chief corner-stone.'

If, then, we are asked why these books of our
Canon are canonical, we must answer that it is
because they are apostolical, and because the Church
is founded upon the apostles.

If we be asked whether this is not such an
acknowledgment of the power of the Church to fix
the Canon as Roman Catholic apologists claim, we
can easily show that it was very different.   By ' the
Church' they mean the organized corporation—in
point of fact, its office-bearers, formally constituted.
Some of them—witness Cardinal Newman[1]—even
go so far as to say that we receive the Canon on
the authority of the Church of the fourth or fifth

---

[1] ' On what ground, then, do we receive the Canon as it comes to us
but on the authority of the Church of the fourth and fifth centuries?
The Church at that era decided—not merely bore testimony, but passed
a judgment on former testimony—that certain books were of authority.
And on what ground did she so decide?   On the ground that a decision

188 RECOGNITION OF AUTHORITY. [LECT. VI.

centuries. But the Church gave no decision during those centuries. There is not in the whole history of the Church of Christ down to the Council of Trent in 1546 any decree or formal utterance of the Church fixing the Canon. There was in Carthage, A.D. 397, a local gathering, what Presbyterians would call a meeting of presbytery, representing forty-four parishes, at which Augustine was present. Its 'decree' speaks of canonical Scriptures, but it does not claim any authority to fix the Canon. It regards 'canonical Scriptures' as already agreed upon, how or when it does not say; and its only concern is to forbid any other books to be read in church under the name of ' Divine Scriptures.' It throws us back to earlier times for the process and the conclusions indicated by its familiar use of the phrase 'canonical Scriptures.' The earlier Council of Laodicea, A.D. 364, has left no genuine decree on the contents of the Canon. We can challenge the Roman Catholic, or any imitator, to point to any authoritative utterance of what he calls ' the Church ' before the Council of Trent. Even if he shared the belief enjoined by recent decrees of the Vatican, and claimed that a pope should speak with church authority, he could find

had been impossible hitherto in an age of persecution from want of opportunities for research, discussion, and testimony ; from the private or the local character of some of the books ; and from misapprehension of the doctrine contained in others.'—NEWMAN, *Development of Christian Doctrine*, p. 125.

on this subject no sure voice of even a pope[1] till about a hundred years before the Tridentine Council, when Pope Eugenius (A.D. 1441) promulgated the same list of books as the Council afterwards sanctioned. There is therefore no acknowledgment of the 'power of the Church' when we accept the New Testament Canon.

Nay more, the whole proceeding is one far removed from conciliar or ecclesiastical authority. When it is seen to be one of authorship, why should a council be needed to settle that? No council of grammarians settled the number of the writings of Cicero or Livy. Each one when it appeared was attested by those who knew; and any man would think it absurd to demand the proof that some literary society in Rome recorded in its minutes the fact of such and such a work (which would have needed to be engrossed in those minutes) having come from the pen of the orator or of the historian. The acceptance of an epistle as Paul's in any branch of the Church was the result of an inquiry and of satisfactory attestation, such as that with which men were familiar every day. No doubt this was only the first step towards canonizing the epistle. But it was the inevitable first step. Once it was taken the next followed. This letter is Paul's,

---

[1] Innocent I. (A.D. 405) is said to have written a letter, but it is not believed to be genuine. The Decree of Gelasius (A.D. 492?) cannot be quoted because of its being subjected to so many alterations. See *Canonicity.*

men said, and thereupon deference to the contents,
obedience to its unhesitating claim, sprang out of
the work of the Spirit of God living in the Church.
' Eye had not seen, nor ear heard, what God had prepared for them that love Him ; but God had revealed
them unto Christian believers by His Spirit,' and
those letters of their apostles were the embodiment
of that divine revelation. We are not transcen-
dental, we are only historical, when we appeal to
the correspondence of the contents of the Epistle
with the spiritual testimony in a believer's heart,
as endowing in those early times the apostolic letter
with its irresistible power. It is to this St. Paul
appeals in his letter to the Galatians : ' I make
known to you, brethren, as touching the gospel
which was preached by me, that it is not after
man. For neither did I receive it from man, nor
was I taught it, but it came to me through revelation of Jesus Christ' (Gal. i. 11, 12). Then he
recalls them to his gospel, and says : ' I am afraid
of you, lest by any means I have bestowed labour
upon you in vain' (iv. 11). ' With freedom did
Christ set us free : stand fast, therefore' (v. 1).
' Ye were running well ; who did hinder you that
ye should not obey the truth ?' (v. 7). One can
easily see how a letter like that, besides the large
characters in which his infirmity of vision caused
him to write all or part of it when he wrote with
his own hand, would bear in its very contents what

waked up the memory of his miracles and his power; and what was therefore an irresistible appeal to the Galatians to bow before it, to count it God's word, to make it the centre and nucleus of their New Testament. I do not refer to that as taking the subject out of the realm of history; on the contrary, these are the historical elements which lead us to accept the Galatian canonization of this letter as an ultimate historical fact.

We have tried to bring the formation of the Canon into the regions of history. And it remains to indicate the kind of historical proof which shows that it was formed in the way we have described, and that this was the principle which ruled men through the ages. We have already incidentally stated the proof when dealing with the testimonies of the early Christians; but we may now collect the principles which these testimonies contain, referring to previous lectures for fuller details. The Muratorian Canon (see before, p. 157) accepts the canonical books as coming from apostles. Books of more recent date than the apostolic era the unknown author summarily rejects; books of heretics, books forged in the names of apostles, he throws away; but the books he accepts are apostolic books. The way in which he connects Luke's Gospel with Paul, and the Acts with Paul and Peter, shows that he did not think Luke had authority to write what took place after Paul and

Peter were removed from his side. And of all the books in his catalogue he implies, what he says of the Gospels, that they come from one Supreme Spirit. The Spirit in the Church had recognised the Spirit speaking in the books.

Irenæus (A.D. 180) founds Christian acceptance of the books on the fact that God made the same men write the books whom He had in the first instance made heralds of the faith.[1]

Tertullian (A.D. 160–220) says : 'We settle it first of all that the evangelical collection (*Evangelicum Instrumentum*) had apostles for its authors, on whom this function of promulgating the gospel was laid by the Lord Himself; and if there were also apostolic men [not apostles], yet they did not stand alone as authors, but wrought with apostles and after apostles.' He goes on to say that the authority of those apostolic men (Mark and Luke) would be liable to suspicion if it were not supported by the authority of their masters.[2] When he speaks of the Epistles he challenges the doubters to go to the churches to which those Epistles were addressed if they wanted the apostolicity of the letters to be authenticated. 'If you are near Achaia, you have Corinth. If you are not far from Macedonia, you have the Philippians, you have the Thessalonians. If you can bend your steps to Asia, you have

---

[1] See Note at end of this lecture.
[2] Tert. *Adv. Marc.* iv. 2; *Canonicity*, p. 76.

Ephesus,' etc.[1]   He thus bases his acceptance upon
the evidence for apostolic authorship of the particular letters which could be had in those churches.
Some think that his words point to the existence of
the originals of the several letters in those places
at his day.   But this is uncertain.

Origen (A.D. 184–253) is satisfied to refer the
writings to apostles, and he dwells upon Mark
writing what Peter recounted, and on Luke's being
the Gospel which Paul praised.[2]   He accepts
Hebrews as Paul's, as all the Eastern Church did,
and accounts for its being more Hellenistic in
phraseology than Paul's ordinary letters are, by
supposing that some Greek like Clement or Luke
wrote it, conveying the pupil's account of his great
master's thoughts.

Eusebius, at his later date (A.D. 270–340), founds
upon the acceptance or rejection by the Church, but
not as though the Church had authority to make a
Canon.   It is only to the historical testimony of the
Church he refers, and that testimony goes to establish the fact of apostolic authorship.   In the previous century we find how Caius and Dionysius
reasoned against the reception of the Apocalypse on
the ground of its not being the work of the Apostle
John.   Caius boldly called it fabricated nonsense,
and ascribed it to Cerinthus.   Dionysius, more

---

[1] *De Præs. Hæret.* c. 36 ; *Canonicity*, p. 48.
[2] Euseb. *H. E.* vi. 25 ; *Canonicity*, p. 8.   See before, p. 165.

cautiously, says he would not venture to set aside a book which many brethren esteem so highly. By 'set aside' he means to scout, and all his arguments tend to put it away as being the work of some unknown author.[1] These men felt that it would not be a canonical book if it were not apostolical.

In the same way the illustrious Athanasius (A.D. 365) wants to set forth the books which have been canonized and handed down (παραδοθέντα) and accredited (πιστευθέντα), *believed* to be divine. He speaks of their acceptance as a long accomplished fact; they are a collection which can neither be made greater nor less. They are the wells of salvation; in them alone is the teaching of piety.[2]

If Cyril of Jerusalem (A.D. 386)[3] dwells upon the living organic connection between the Old Testament and the New, it is not to supersede his confidence in the agreement to which the Church had come upon the numbers and the names of the books.

Jerome (A.D. 329–420), too, founds upon the consent of past ages. He dwells on the inner glory of the Scriptures; but not as though that were in lieu of the historical argument. 'Matthew, Mark, Luke, and John, the four-steed chariot of the Lord and the true cherubim (a word which means the manifoldness of wisdom), have eyes over their whole

---

[1] See *Canonicity*, p. 343, for Caius; and pp. 346, 347, for Dionysius.

[2] Athanasius' Paschal Letter (39). See *Canonicity*, p. 13.

[3] *Catechis.* iv. 36; *Canonicity*, p. 19.

bodies; they shower out sparks, lightnings glow all round them, their feet are erect and mount on high, their backs are winged and fly everywhere. They are interlaced, too, and all their movements are as though wheel were within wheel, and they go wherever the breath of the Holy Spirit guides them.' And at the close of his enumeration of the books he says: 'My words are inadequate to the worth of the volume. All laudation is beneath its desert; in every single word there lie multiplied meanings.'[1]

⌣In Augustine (A.D. 354–430) we find a more simple acceptance of ancient testimonies, but they are the testimonies of the central Christian churches; and he thus repeats the principle of Tertullian.[2] The so-called 'Apostolical Constitutions' require that readers not only take note of apostolical names attached to books, but of the nature of the contents.[3]

In short, it can be made out that early Christians, knowing that the apostles were accredited by Christ to be the founders of the Church, accepted the books because proved to come from those apostles, and never raised any other test in regard to any one of which they were in doubt unless it be this—that it should harmonize with those of which they were already sure. In that way they used the apostolic

[1] *Epist.* ii. *ad Paulinum; Canonicity*, p. 21.
[2] *De Doctrina Christiana*, ii. 12, 13; *Canonicity*, p. 20.
[3] *Apost. Constt.* vi. 16; *Canonicity*, p. 26.

books already in their hands to test others which
were brought to their notice.

During the centuries which intervene between
the Council of Nice (A.D. 325) and the Reformation,
there is not much to cause us to tarry in our historical survey.   Lists of canonical books, compiled
by individuals, are common enough.   Two are
ascribed to popes, but without good reason.   Nor
is there much to cause delay when we search for
the principles on which, during that period, canonical authority was ascribed to the books of the
New Testament.   Christendom was built on the
apostles and prophets, and occupied itself in raising
and extending the goodly edifice ; often enough
putting wood, hay, and stubble on the living stones
of the sure foundation.   In the fifteenth century,
when the corruptions of the Church were becoming
intolerable, men began again to search and see
what manner of basis there was for the Christian
faith.   In that terrible confusion, when at one time
there were four rival popes and at another two,
each of the latter with a council to sustain him,
when Huss was burnt for heresy by a judgment
which came from a profligate pope, there were
many signs that men were inquiring after the true
word of God.   Wiclif's work was spreading and
making men think.   Pope Eugenius, in A.D. 1441,
broke the long silence of the Church by promulgating, on his own authority, a list of the books of

Scripture, a list which was faithfully echoed by the
Council of Trent a hundred years later.   This was
not an authoritative list, for the Romish Church
had by this time concluded that it is not the pope
alone, but the pope in council, that is infallible.

As regards the New Testament, the papal list
is the same as our own ; but because the Latin
Vulgate, Jerome's translation of the Scripture, contained the Old Testament Apocrypha, the decree
of the pope, and eventually of the council, must
needs canonize the whole.   It was not easy for the
Romish Church to own that it had erred so long
in accepting those apocryphal books ; and ignorant
ecclesiastics directed this Canon of the Vulgate,
and apparently the Latin translation itself, to be
acknowledged as the ultimate authority in 'public
readings, discussions, preachings, and expositions.'
The Tridentine Council furthermore forbade any
one to dare to interpret Scripture 'contrary to that
sense which the Holy Mother Church has held and
holds, . . . even though such interpretations should
never be destined to come to light.'   The necessity
of finding some means of putting down Luther
and the Reformers led the Latin Church to this
restrictive and irrational use of the Vulgate and
its Canon.   The Church furthermore resolved to
have an authoritative edition of this standard
Canon, and one was published with the full weight
of papal approval, which, however, was so full of

blunders as to be superseded two years afterwards
by another that no scholar regards as infallible,
though it is better than its predecessor.

Thus the Bible of the Romish Church contains
as part of its Canon those apocryphal books which
were not acknowledged as scriptural by our Lord
or by any of His apostles ; and it is, moreover, a
translation not admitted to be dependent on the
sacred originals, through which the word of God
came to man at first. It is little wonder that a
Church which could digest a decree like that should
have been found competent in our later times to
promulgate the personal infallibility of the pope
and the immaculate birth of the Virgin Mary.
When Erasmus said,[1] in his usual solemn mockery,
that as a man he could not see the Pauline
authorship of Hebrews, but that as a son of
the Church he accepted it, he was only furnishing a formula of which the morbid earnestness
of John Henry Newman [2] makes pathetic use

[1] 'Juxta sensum humanum nec credo Ep. ad Hebr. esse Pauli aut
Lucæ, nec secundam Petri esse Petri, nec Apocalypsim esse Joannis Ap.
qui scripsit Evangelium.' But if the Church has received the titles as
well as the books, 'Id si est, damno dubitationem meam . . . plus apud
me valet expressum Ecclesiæ judicium quam ullæ rationes humanæ'
(Declar. ad censur. Fac. Theol. Paris. Opp. ix. 864). Again, of Hebrews
he says: 'Ipse, ut ingenue fatear, adhuc dubito, non de auctoritate, sed
de auctore' (Supputatio errorum N. Beddæ, ix. 595).

[2] See Newman's Apologia pro Vita Mea, and his Development of
Christian Doctrine, passim. The latter work is even more interesting
than the Apologia, because it gives the actual arguments which the
author was weighing when the necessary conclusion forced itself upon
him, so that before the book was all printed he acted upon it and left

in regard to all popish dogmas in our nineteenth century.

The Greek Church meanwhile had not made such free use as the Roman Church had made of extra-canonical books in her daily worship, although admitting that some of them were good for edifying. There was a formal decree on the subject by the Council of Laodicea, A.D. 364, which said, 'That except canonical Scriptures, nothing should be read in church under the name of Divine Scriptures.' There is a spurious addition to this decree, giving a list of canonical books; but the genuine decree ends with the words we have quoted. The Trullan Council of Constantinople, A.D. 692, confirmed the Laodicean decrees, but we are not entitled to say that the list of books was among those adopted. Those who pin their faith to those two councils do a daring thing, for the Laodicean was a local synod, probably an Arian one, and even the Trullan was not a general council, and the Romish Church does not admit it.

Thus the Eastern Church was as completely without a fixed Canon as the Western at the Reformation. This fact induced Cyril Lukar, the great patriarch of Alexandria and afterwards of Constantinople, who had spent some years in Europe among the Reformers, to believe that he

the Church of England. The ambiguity lurking in the word 'church' has always caused the gifted and venerated author to mistake the leading of the 'Kindly Light.'

could prevail upon his Church not only to avoid the Romish error of canonizing the Apocrypha, but to adopt the Protestant principle of magnifying Scripture above tradition and above the Church. In his sanguine hopefulness he published a noble document, 'A Confession of the Faith of the Greek Church of the East,' in which he denied all authority to the apocryphal books, because 'they derive none from the Holy Spirit;' but, on the other hand, exalted the position of Holy Scripture as coming direct from God, as being higher than the Church, as being a plain book from which all regenerate men of every grade could draw the infallible wisdom and the everlasting power they need.[1] He adopted the list of books ascribed to the Council of Laodicea, quietly adding, however, the Apocalypse. Instead of the cordial acceptance or even quiet acquiescence on which the good patriarch had counted, the whole Church of the East rose in commotion against him and his 'Calvinism;' men scouted the idea of the ancient East being reformed by petty Geneva; and when they had put Cyril to death with a bowstring in the Bosphorus, his enemies called a council to promulgate a true Confession of the Eastern Faith. Its chief purpose was to exalt the Church as equal to Scripture, and to declare that the apocryphal

---

[1] Cyr. *Catech.* chap. ii. quest. 1; Kimmel's *Lib. Symbol. Eccl. Or.* pp. 25, 40, 42.

books have as much right to be counted Holy
Scripture as any others have, and that Cyril, who
had thought otherwise, was without sense or learning, and a man bent on doing ill.[1]   This Council of
Jerusalem (1672), in adopting the Confession and
Catechism of Dositheos, which contained the foregoing among many other notable remarks, was
probably for two hundred years representative of
the views of the Eastern Church—though that
Church has always had more freedom, less cohesion,
and less confession than the Church of Rome ; but
in our own day a catechism which is the work of
the Metropolitan of Moscow, and under the pat-
ronage of the Russian Emperor, has altered the
state of things for the better.   This catechism of
Philaret, A.D. 1839, does indeed exalt tradition as
the voice of the living Church and as a guide to
the understanding of the Scripture, but nevertheless holds that it is only to be followed so far as it
agrees with the divine revelation and with Holy
Scripture.   It further makes Scripture indispensable for securing the unchangeableness of revelation ; and it cuts the Apocrypha adrift by declaring
that the Old Testament Canon contains the twenty-
two Hebrew books, and the New Testament the
twenty-seven accepted by Athanasius.   In short,
it accepts a Canon identical with our own.[2]

---

[1] Dositheos' *Conf.* quest. 3.   See *Canonicity*, p. 34.
[2] Schaff, *Creeds*, p. 445.

Thus, then, at this moment, the Greek Church
accepts the Bible without the Apocrypha, and puts
the Scripture above the Church. The Romish
Church puts the Apocrypha in the Bible, and rests
the authority and the interpretation of the Canon
on the voice of the Church.

What is the position of the reformed Churches ?[1]
The Reformers did not at first concern themselves
with the Canon. They were occupied with doctrine,
and they found the doctrine in the books accepted
by the Romish Church as by themselves. But
they did not enumerate the books; still less did
they think of saying why they believed them to be
divine. Thus the sixty-seven articles of Zwingli
(1523) have no paragraph on the Canon; and the
same is true of the Theses of Berne (1528).[2] The
Genevan Catechism (1536, expanded 1545) has no
article on the Scripture. Even when Scripture
came to be spoken of more definitely, there was
still no list of the books which make up Scripture.
The Swiss, the German, and the old Scottish Confessions contain no list of the books of the Bible.
We find one in the French Confession (Calvin's
work) of 1559; and another in the Belgian
Confession of 1561, revised in 1619.

---

[1] See a more detailed examination of the views of the Reformers in
an article on 'Canonicity,' in the *British and Foreign Evangelical Review*,
1870. The substance of what follows is the same as in that article,
though I have tried to avoid repetition.

[2] This document only says that its conclusions are drawn from the
biblical writings of the Old and New Testaments.

In both the last - named creeds there is an assault on the Roman Church, in a distinct claim of supremacy for Holy Scriptures, on the ground that the testimony and inward illumination of the Holy Spirit enables Christians to distinguish it from all other ecclesiastical books. The Council of Trent had formally thrown down a challenge. It recognised the Canon because of the traditions of the Church, and on the same ground of tradition accepted the unwritten ideas about Christ and His apostles, of which the Church had been made the custodian. The Reformers believed Scripture to be higher than the Church. But on what could they rest their acceptance of the Canon of Scripture? How did they know those books to be Holy Scriptures, the only and ultimate divine revelation? They answered that the divine authority of Scripture is self-evidencing, that the regenerate man needs no other evidence, and that only the regenerate can appreciate the evidence. It follows from this that if he do not feel the evidence of their contents, any man may reject books claiming to be Holy Scripture. The Reformers did not attempt to deal with the obviously possible and probable case of a man who, though regenerate, is only partially enlightened, and who naturally, though wrongly, rejects books which he cannot understand. But they did proclaim in trumpet tones their wide

severance from the Latin Church, which appealed
to the witness of the Holy Spirit in the office-
bearers of the Church, while the Churches of the
Reformation appealed to the witness of the Holy
Spirit in the individual heart.   The Church disappeared; the personal conviction was all in all.
They thought that in this way they made doctrine
the test of the books as the early Church was
enjoined to do (Gal. i. 9; 2 Thess. ii. 1; 1 John iv. 1).

We may quote Luther's well-known words:
'The touchstone is when one sees whether a book
urges Christ on him or no; what does not teach
Christ is not apostolical, no, not though Paul or
Peter taught it; while, on the other hand, what
preaches Christ would be apostolical, even though
Judas, or Annas, or Pilate, or Herod did it'
(Preface to James).   Elsewhere he says: 'In short,
John's Gospel and his First Epistle, the Epistles
of Paul,—especially those to Romans, Galatians,
and Ephesians,—and Peter's First Epistle, these
are the books which show thee Christ, and teach
thee all that it is holy and needful to know,
though thou shouldst never see nor hear the teaching of another book' (Preface to New Testament).
This bold severance of the doctrine from the
apostle who taught it, is entirely contrary to the
mode of judging seen in the Christians of the
apostolic times, if we have apprehended their judgment rightly.   To Luther the apostle was nothing;

to the Christians of the first age the apostle was everything. St. Paul's sweeping anathema on man or angel who should preach another gospel than his, was merely his way of saying that his gospel was God's message, and divinely true for ever.

Luther's translation bore witness to his thoroughness in applying his principle. He set Hebrews, James, Jude, and the Apocalypse at the end of the New Testament; attaching no numbers to them, while he had numbered the previous twenty-three books, and at the close of the twenty-three, saying: 'Thus far have we the right and certain chief books of the New Testament.' Although he glanced at the lack of ancient testimony to those books, he did not hide his objections to them on doctrinal grounds. Against Hebrews he brings forward its denial of repentance after baptism; against James (an 'Epistle of mere straw'), the opposition to Paul, and the attempt to teach Christianity without once mentioning the sufferings of Christ; against Jude, its being a superfluous echo of Second Peter; while of the Apocalypse he says: 'My spirit cannot enter into that book; and it is reason enough for my not holding it in high esteem that Christ is neither recognised nor taught in it.'[1]

It is obvious that this position was liable to assault on many sides. Luther himself was

---

[1] This denunciation of the Apocalypse was afterwards modified.

embarrassed by the claims of the Mystics. They, like him, said the inner spirit was all-important; but unlike him, they claimed to have a higher illumination than the written word. He tried to show that no Mystic is warranted to contradict the general testimony of the Spirit in the disciples of Christ; but he felt that in consequence he must modify some of his own strong statements regarding the four books he had cast out. He was too resolute, and felt himself too right, to withdraw his general principle.

Nor indeed could he have withdrawn it. It was in the air. The other Reformers were full of it, like himself. Zwingli claimed the right to reject the testimonies which might be adduced for the Apocalypse, inasmuch as 'it did not (to him) smack of the mouth and spirit of John.' The hearts of the Reformers were burdened with the obligation to proclaim as a primary truth that the soul of man has direct communion with the living God; and they could not but hold and teach that God so speaks to man in the word, that the word interprets itself to every willing soul. But they erred in speaking as though they were the discoverers of Scripture. In one sense they were: they had found it deep down beneath rubbish and wrong; but, in a higher sense, it had been God's bread for hungering souls through all ages. They knew that Christ was with them as they read and prayed; but they forgot that He had been always with His own.

Calvin felt the force of such considerations, for his writings and the creeds of the Churches which he swayed give a place to the historical evidence for the books of the Canon.[1]   He asserts as strongly as Luther that Scripture itself is the best evidence that it has come from God; but he does not stop there, so as to cast away every testimony that does not rise up in the individual heart.   He meets those who asked how they could be persuaded that Scripture has come from God, unless they take refuge in a decree of the Church, by asking them in return how they knew light from darkness and sweet from bitter, and by declaring that Scripture brings a perception of its own truth. But he does not forget that the consent of the Church is to be kept in mind, as well as the intellectual arguments for the divine character of the Bible, when a man who has the inner witness looks for arguments such as can be used to convince others.[2]

The testimony of the Reformers seems to us faulty from defect; but it is needful to clear it of some misconceptions.   It is often said of them

[1] Though Calvin does not admit that Peter is the author of the Second Epistle in his name, or that Paul wrote Hebrews, he comes to his conclusion on historical grounds. Luther sometimes did so also; e.g. he says Jude never needed Greek, as he went to Persia, so that the Epistle cannot be his.

[2] Calv. *Inst.* Book I. chaps. vi. vii. viii.

that they substituted the Infallible Book for the
Infallible Man ; so that—quite as much as Papists
—they were under an infallibility which took their
own responsibility away.   But this is not at all a
true account.   The fundamental principle of the
Reformation was that a sinner has direct, saving,
and indestructible communion with the living
God.   In the matter of the Canon, this led to
the transfer of authority from the witness of the
Spirit in the visible Church to the witness of the
Spirit in the regenerate heart.   The test of all
truth, the test of the warrant of each book to be
accepted as canonical, was, according to the first
Reformers,   the   witness   of   the   Christian   soul
instructed by the Holy Spirit of Jesus Christ
Himself.   Luther and Zwingli found the infallible
authority in the Spirit of God within themselves.
This is indeed open to challenge, but not on the
ground that it substituted an infallible Church for
an infallible man.   Its weakness is that it isolated
the individual Christian.

When Calvin gave a place to historical testimony,
he effected a revolution, though its effects were
not seen for a long time.   When he enumerates
the arguments for the authority of Scripture,
such as the nature of the doctrine, the exquisite
harmony of the different parts, the antiquity of
the books, the miraculous sanctions of the law,
the evidence of prophecy, and winds up his

enumeration with the 'consent of the Church,'
he was manifesting his usual independence and far-
sightedness. In his view, Scripture is undoubtedly
and essentially self-evidencing (αὐτόπιστος) when the
Holy Spirit is teaching a human soul, but nevertheless human testimonies are valuable accessories
to the primary foundation.

It is in the nature of things that this admission
of historical testimony should become more avowed
and prominent as we trace the stream of events
from Calvin's days to our own. The Churches of
the Reformation were, like Christendom itself,
based upon doctrine and fact before they had
books for standards; and the bond of union
among them was the Protestant doctrine which
they held. Naturally and logically, they omitted
from their creeds at first any list of the canonical
writings. In course of time, however, and under
the influences of controversy, they were led to
intimate their adherence to a fixed Canon. From
the same causes they came, in subsequent times,
to accept on no higher authority than tradition
the canonical Scripture as supreme in all controversy. The ordinary faith of Christians appears
until a comparatively recent date to have been
expressed by the practical yet self-contradictory
words of the Articles of the Church of England
(1562), which say in one place, like the Confession
of Würtemberg and the Belgian Confession, that

the Canon is limited to those books 'of whose authority there never was any doubt in the Church,' and in another that it consists of 'all the books as they were commonly received at the Reformation.' The Würtemberg Confession excludes the Antilegomena from its list, and thus secures consistency, but the English Article includes them. Such a position cannot bear close examination, for the most cursory glance shows that there are some books in our Canon of which there was much doubt in the Church, notably at the time of the Reformation. Again, Luther put four books in an inferior rank, while the Anglican Church makes no distinction. The Anglican Articles, moreover, make no mention of the grounds upon which the Reformers accepted certain books. The conclusion, in short, rests upon no principle, and is merely an acceptance of limited and recent tradition. It must be added that the Church of England gives no list of books of the New Testament which are to be received into the Canon, and so increases the perplexity into which her utterances on the subject have put her members.

The Confession of the Westminster Divines is in a different relation to science. It bases the authority of Scripture solely on its being the Word of God; and the proof of its being the Word of God is divided into many parts, of which the 'testimony of the Church' is the first, and the 'incomparable excellences and the entire perfection' of the Scripture itself is the last; 'yet, notwithstanding, our full persuasion and assurance of the infallible truth and divine authority thereof is from the inward work of the Holy Spirit, bearing witness by and with the Word in our hearts.'

Here there is every branch of the wide argument. The external testimony from old time, the appeal to our intellect made by the unspeakable grandeur of the Word of God, the appeal to our conscience from the 'efficacy of the doctrine,' and the discovery of the way of salvation ; but finally, and above all, the inward work of the Holy Spirit enabling the child of God to be sure that he hears his Father's voice.

Such a combination of various considerations is the only possible mode of arriving at a sure and adequate conclusion. Science, history, and inner light are not mutual foes, but allies in behalf of truth ; and men who shut out any one of them are not true to the wide veracity of the revelation of God.

For let us see how we may state our reasons for accepting the Bible as the Word of God.

I. Those reasons are not merely *objective*, like those stated by some Churches.

(1.) They are not those of the Roman Catholic

Church. They do not, like Cardinal Newman's, peril all upon the voice of the Church, so that we should be bound to accept any dogma whatever which the Church may choose to promulgate, on the same grounds as we take the Bible on the Church's authority. We do not deny the fascination which Papists and Plymouthists feel in the truth of a living Church whose life is the indwelling Holy Spirit; but we do not believe that the life of the Church can be true if it develops outside of the truth of the Word.

(2.) They are not those of the Greek Church. We neither agree with Dositheos in 1672, that because of ancient tradition we must take the Apocrypha as part of Holy Scripture, nor with Philaret in 1839, that holy tradition is in any sense or degree co-ordinate with Holy Scripture. We do not think that—apart from Scripture—the Church has proved herself a 'sure repository of holy tradition.'

(3.) Our reasons are not those of the Articles of the Church of England. They cannot be, because those Articles give reasons inconsistent with each other and with history.

All these are merely objective. They appeal blindly to an outer Church. They do not take into account that, as matters of fact, the corporate Church of the West never formally fixed the Canon till the sixteenth century, and that of the

East did not follow its example till a hundred years afterwards.

II. But, on the other hand, our reasons are not wholly *subjective*.

(1.) We cannot agree with the first Reformers, who took no account of the general voice of Christendom, and acted as though each solitary man were brought to weigh the claims of a new book. Luther, and those who agreed with him, debarred the individual from taking into consideration the historical testimony of Christ's people and the contemporary personal testimonies of all awakened men, and thus magnified the Christian to the exclusion of Christendom. The living Church, which was founded upon and built up in Jesus Christ, ceased to have any evidence in its origin or in its history for the books of Scripture.

(2.) We cannot agree with Coleridge that only in so far as there is in the Bible what 'finds him' is it God's word for him. For is there no rightful authority in the Bible if a man be so lost or so dull that he does not feel it? Or may a man refuse to admit that there is any evidence for the word of God being found in those parts which do not find *him?* This seems to be Coleridge's position.[1]

---

[1] See Coleridge's *Confessions of an Inquiring Spirit*, Letters i. and ii. This touching, beautiful, and suggestive work receives great injustice when it is supposed to be a plagiarism from Lessing. The German was the advocate of intellect; Coleridge was a devout, 'inquiring spirit.' His

The Bible is to be simply tried by a subjective test.

A similar objection applies to the kindred view held by many, and by none more beautifully expressed than by the late eminent historian Dean Milman. It is to the effect that while humanity retains its needs and cravings, it must have the religion of the Bible ; and—though that was not the aim of the great historian—the result is to leave us in doubt whether man did not invent the religion which he thus needs.[1]

argument seems to me to be defective ; but no theory of the authority of Scripture can be adequate which does not embrace the powerful argument suggested by Coleridge in many wonderfully beautiful passages in those Confessions. I quote two : 'And need I say that I have met everywhere more or less copious sources of truth, and power, and purifying impulses ; that I have found words for my inmost thoughts, songs for my joy, utterances for my hidden griefs, and pleadings for my shame and my feebleness' (Letter i.). 'But let me once be persuaded that . . . the royal harper, to whom I have so often submitted myself as a many-stringed instrument for his fire-tipt fingers to traverse, while every several nerve of emotion, passion, thought, that thrids the flesh and blood of our common humanity, responded to the touch, was himself as mere an instrument as his harp, an *automaton* poet, mourner, and supplicant ;—all is gone,—all sympathy, at least, and all example. I listen in awe and fear, but likewise in perplexity and confusion of spirit' (Letter iii.). Coleridge was endeavouring to overturn the mechanical theory of inspiration, according to which (apparently) the humanity of the inspired man was paralyzed for the time being. But his reaction is too complete when his own theory is merely this: 'In short, whatever *finds* me, bears witness for itself that it has proceeded from a Holy Spirit' (Letter i.). For though this is excellent, it cannot be all.

[1] 'For the perpetuity of religion, of the true religion, that of Christ, I have no misgivings. So long as there are women and sorrow in this mortal world, so long will there be the religion of the *emotions*, the religion of the affections. Sorrow will have consolations which it can only find in the gospel. So long as there is a sense of goodness, the sense of the misery and degradation of evil, there will be the religion of what we

Every theory which begins in the denial of
authority to the Bible as being God's word, is
logically bound to end in setting the intuitions of
man above what we believe to be the written revelation. Not the intuitions of the renewed man
only, as Luther would have it, but the intuitions of
man. I regret to find the most striking instance
of this in the case of a man now venerable in years,
as he has long been conspicuous for gifts of intellect
and graces of style, and a wonderful sympathy with
the upward strivings of human hearts. In an address
delivered a few months ago, Dr. James Martineau,
trying to estimate the 'Loss and Gain in Recent
Theology,' casts off all appearance of regard for the
authority of Scripture. He says : 'Consider first
the total disappearance from our branch of the
Reformed Churches of all *external authority* in
matters of religion. The conception of a canonical literature that shall serve as a divine statute-

---

may call the *moral necessities* of our nature, the yearning for rescue from
sin, for reconciliation with an All-Holy God. So long as the spiritual
wants of our higher being require an authoritative answer, so long as the
human mind cannot but conceive its imaginative, discursive, creative,
inventive thought to be something more than a mere faculty or innate
or acquired power of the material body ; so long as there are aspirations
towards immortality, so long as man has a conscious soul, and feels that
soul to be his real self—his imperishable self,—so long will there be the
religion of *reason*. As it was the moral and religious superiority of
Christianity, in other words, the love of God diffused by Christ, "by
God in Christ," which mainly subdued and won the world, so that same
power will retain it in willing and perpetual subjection. The strength
of Christianity will rest not in the exalted imagination, but in the heart,
the conscience, the understanding of man.'—MILMAN, *History of Christianity*, Preface, p. xxii.

book belongs to a stage of culture that has passed
away.' 'The perennial fountains of religion lie in
the deepest wells of our nature, in the primary
essence of the reason and the moral consciousness.'

And again he sums up thus : 'The Bible neither
is nor professes to be a creed and code ; we have
therefore no authoritative text-book of divine truth
and human duty, so we must open our minds
to all that speaks divinely to them, whether in the
Bible or elsewhere.'

It may be a comfort to him to be ' delivered to
the intuitions and pieties of our nature,' but most of
us are thankful, as David said, that there is a
revealed law of the Lord which 'converteth the
soul, and maketh wise the simple.' Most of us are
thankful to have been taught the prayer, 'Sanctify
us through the truth : Thy word is truth.' The
aged Unitarian minister has long been to many—as
Channing was—a proof that a man may be better
than his creed, a proof that a man may love the
word, and even the Word made flesh, though his
creed be cold and comfortless Socinianism ; but he
now demands to be regarded as the head of a
number of moralists proclaiming 'the disappearance
from their faith of the entire *Messianic mythology.*'
Let us hope that few of those who, in their
' Endeavours after the Christian Life,' have had
him for their guide, will follow him thus far !

III. I cannot agree with another theory which goes farther than the Reformers and Coleridge, taking other living men into account, but *gives little weight to the argument from history.* The best statement of this position is found in the writings of the late Professor Beck of Tübingen. It is based upon Calvin and Luther, but as a whole is, as might be expected, independent. It is interesting as containing the core of the teaching which for so many decades attracted the largest theological class in Germany, and in Tübingen itself drew crowds of students away from Baur. It is to the effect that, while external testimonies are all very well in their own place, they must never be exalted into proofs of the Scriptures containing a divine revelation; for that the Scripture contains in itself a divinely working spiritual power which is its own best evidence. When the Bible was given, the miraculous revelation out of which the writings came was the essential element in the spiritual condition of the divine kingdom that was ruling men. The men of that day had their function in connection with Scripture, and it was discharged. But we are in very different circumstances. We have not to begin to search and see if among all the books in the world there be any which are Holy Scripture. We in our time have to deal with the fact that we are in the middle of a believing community, whose belief in revelation is a belief in

certain Scriptures as containing that revelation.
To us, therefore, the question is whether those
Scriptures verify their claim, and justify their place,
by producing the same divine spiritual results as
they undertake to produce. Do those Scriptures
justify themselves as God's word to man ? Are
they still full of spirit and power ? That they
are, all spiritual men testify. In all ages the
Scripture has legitimized itself by the immanence
of a life-giving Spirit ; and at this moment the
Scripture is always the producing element, while
man is the receptive and reproductive, so that it
was not only God-breathed when first written,
but even now God breathes through the Scripture
while man reads it, and the Scripture itself breathes
life. It follows from this that we should not need
to distress ourselves if apocryphal books, or other
candidates for a place as inspired writings, were
to be brought forward, because, until they could
show for themselves that they produced those
spiritual results, they need not occupy attention.
On the other hand, each individual book of Scripture is an integral part of the organic whole of
Scripture, and the general conscience of the
spiritual people of Christ attests that it is. An
individual here and there may be unable to
recognise the Spirit of God in a book, as Luther
was for long when dealing with the Apocalypse
and the Epistle of James, but the great community

of the members of Christ's body are not so defective in spiritual enlightenment or so one-sided. What the exceptional individual does not recognise is full of life to others, and thus the Spirit which dwells in spiritual people as a whole, attests each and every book of the New Testament.[1] Thus the ultimate test of the canonicity of a book is not a mere weighing of historical testimonies, nor a subjective inner witness from personal feelings and conception of the truth, because no mere mental test can comprehend the Spirit of God, but a spiritual criticism, in which every thought ($\pi\hat{\alpha}\nu$ $\nu\acute{o}\eta\mu\alpha$) is brought into subjection to the faith (2 Cor. x. 5), and in which there is a power of spiritually recognising the truth in God's word, judging Scripture by Scripture in the very spirit of the Scripture itself. Like Calvin and Bengel, Professor Beck will not allow the judgments of unregenerate men to be of the slightest moment in contributing to the all-important decision.

In this noble and consistent scheme, which was the centre of the life-thought of one of the most potent theologians of our time, there seems to me to be this defect, that it takes too little account of history. For the mass of Christian people it is ample, but it would leave to the enemy the whole field of historical criticism. It was a needed reaction, but too great a reaction from the cold

[1] See Beck, *Einleitung in das System der christlichen Lehre,* §§ 82–101.

historical survey of Baur. If we can correct the
individual aberrations of Luther by the general
testimony of the contemporary people of God,
why should we shut out from our survey the
whole general testimony of the bygone ages which
are embalmed for us in history ?

IV. *Our answer, then, is partly objective and partly
subjective, partly present, partly historical.* There
are before us two great facts which Coleridge
called the primary evidences of Christianity, viz.
Christianity itself and Christendom. We know
nothing like them ; nothing with claims, nothing
with achievements, like theirs. We find that they
both rest on this Book ; both find their verification
in it. It came out from their bosom ; they return
to it evermore for their strength and warrant ;
for it contains the truth of God, out of which
they grew, and to which, as contained in it, they
testified when it appeared. It is the work of the
men whom God sent forth to teach all nations,
and to make disciples of all men ; and its truth
is still as great and living as when they spoke it
and wrote it.

In that Book, when our souls are opened to
receive it, we find a revelation of God which all
that is best in us bows before, and which also
the demon-part of us acknowledges while trying
to think that we have nothing to do with Jesus,
the Son of the Most High God. It brings life

and immortality to light—a light which is brighter
than all others, as the blaze which smote Paul
to the ground was brighter than the rays of the
Syrian sun at noon. Above all, we find in it the
Person of Jesus Christ, whom we need no outer
proof from any quarter to show to be the chief
among ten thousand, and altogether lovely. The
Person of Jesus Christ is Divine, is God and Man;
and eye never saw, ear never heard, the heart of
man never conceived, a life like that, until ONE
actually dwelt among men and lived it. Not a
dream, nor a myth, nor a fiction, nor exaggeration
of loving discipleship, is this to me, but the very
truth of the living God, the Father in heaven.
All saints that have lived and struggled unto
victory; all martyrs that have triumphed in their
death; all poor penitents that have heard the
voice of hope, and therefore climbed the eternal
altar-stairs that slope through darkness up to
God; all sages that have revered Christ's greater
wisdom; the Church, whose one foundation is
Jesus Christ, her Lord, —all bring us evidence
that the Bible, which is the Book of Jesus Christ,
is the very word of God.

We have learned in our own life that when
we ceased to take our daily portion from its
boundless stores, we became weak and fell; that
all our worst days have come of neglect of
prayerful study of that word for ourselves; that

our corruption always rises when we cease to look
on the Divine Ideal, and so to learn how unfathom-
ably deep and disgraceful that corruption is.   And
what we have found in ourselves, we have seen in
others.   We have seen God's word vindicated in
many a life sanctified by its truth.   We have seen
passion quenched, degradation recalled, despair
dispelled, death himself subjugated, by a simple
faith taught of God.

My friends, the vision is shut up and the
Book is sealed.   No hope has been given us that
the seals will be broken, or a new page added.
Hebrew seers knew that a day of fuller light
would come, and they were on tiptoe for the
coming of the Prophet, the Priest, and the King.
But now that He has come, what more can be
done unto the vineyard?   It was the Lord of
the vineyard's last means : 'I will send my Son.'

But the closed Book is a living word.   Still
as mighty to us as to those of old time is the
'dignity of a saying fresh - descended from the
porch of heaven.'   It will write its witness in your
hearts and lives if ye be true men ; if your eye
is single, its light will fill your body ; if your
heart is pure, you will see God in this Book.
You will see it in the lives and deaths of other
men.   It is the unfolding and revelation of God's
nature, and therefore of all the principles of life.
It is the key to history, the bond of society, as

well as the guide-book of the perplexed and the hope of the fallen. It gives the basis of morals in the living relation of man to the Supreme Father, who is of His own nature holy. And thus comes the supreme authority of the Scriptures: 'They are they which testify of ME.'

DRS. DIESTEL AND ROBERTSON SMITH ON IRENÆUS AND THE RULE OF FAITH.

DIESTEL, in his *Geschichte des Alten Testaments in der christlichen Kirche* (1869), speaks of the difficulty felt by the fathers in finding something fixed to serve as a rule when allegorical interpretations were making the meaning of Scripture vague and shadowy. Allegory was a two-edged sword, opening a door to heresy on the one hand, while closing it on the other. ' And so,' says Diestel, ' one had to grip as a master-key that apostolical tradition in which he saw the universal Christian spirit in its full purity' (p. 38). In this, as in much else, the testimony of Irenæus is of primary importance, inasmuch as he is the author of the earliest extant systematic treatise on Christian theology. Diestel accordingly, after saying that he who sought the master-key of apostolical tradition sought it in the ' Rule of Faith' which was found in the substance of the Exposition of the Church, goes on : ' Irenæus (iv. 25 (26), 2) refers directly to the presbyters " who (he says), along with the succession of the Episcopate, received the sure *charisma* of truth according to the good pleasure of the fathers. . . . For they expound the Scriptures without danger to us, neither blaspheming God, nor dishonouring the patriarchs, nor contemning the prophets." . . . To Irenæus, therefore, the Scripture is the treasure hid in the field (*Adv. Hær.* iv. 25, 26); the laity may read it under the guidance of the presbyters (iv. 32).'

It is scarcely possible, in short compass, to show fully how partial, and therefore misleading, this professed outline of the views of Irenæus is. But *First,* Irenæus does not say that Scripture is the treasure hid in the field ; what he does say, is that Christ is the treasure once hid in the field ; that the treasure was revealed when Christ came; that the Jewish law, when read in the light of His cross, becomes a treasure enriching the understanding, so that men of understanding shine as the brightness of the firmament (Dan. xii. 3). *Second,* Irenæus does not mean to say (as Diestel insinuates) that Scripture can only be read under presbyterial supervision. What he says is that many men, professing to be guides,—' and believed by many to be presbyters,'—are ' men who serve their own lusts,' and ' do not set the fear of God supreme in their own hearts;' that such men are the evil servants whom the Lord when He cometh shall cut in sunder and appoint them a portion with the unbelievers (Matt. xxiv. 48). He therefore exhorts his readers to adhere to those who are the ' guardians of the doctrine of the apostles,' and who have *those two qualifications*, viz. the order of the presbyterate, and along with it, a sound and blameless life. Irenæus is expanding the statements and warnings of Paul to Timothy and Titus. He is proclaiming the principle by which Clement and Origen so strongly held, and which the Reformers afterwards made their own, that no man can be a competent expositor of the word of God who has not the grace of God in his heart ruling the life. It is not enough to be a presbyter; the teacher must also be a man of God. The very sentence of which Diestel quotes a part—as though it were (like the first words) from § 2 of Irenæus, iv. c. 26 (whereas it is from § 5)—is a disproof of his allegation, and proves what we have said. We give it in full, translating also the sentence immediately preceding it: ' Where, therefore, the *charismata* of God are, there ought the truth to be learned, among the men who have the succession of the church which is from the apostles, and in whom is a sound and blameless conversation with untainted and incorruptible speech. For those men both guard our faith towards one God, the Maker of all; and also augment our love towards the Son of God, who accomplished such mighty plans for our sakes; they expound the Scriptures without danger to us, neither blaspheming God, nor dishonouring the patriarchs, nor contemning the prophets.' The mere ' succession ' is not all; there must be also the qualification of special inner grace, by which the teachers increase the faith and the love of their disciples. The passage (iv. 32) to which Diestel further refers, as though it were a Papal prohibition of Bible-reading, is a further warning against the people trusting to teachers who (as being really, though not avowedly, Gnostics) attempted to show that the ' Two Testaments' are in antagonism, and he tells them that they ' will find it all clear if they will diligently read the Scriptures in company with those who are presbyters in the Church, and who *have the apostolic doctrine*, according to the principles we have laid down.'

The evil of such general statements as those of Diestel is still better seen when they are made more sweeping, as they are by his followers, who trust to his induction of facts. Dr. Robertson Smith, in his *Old Testament in the Jewish Church*, has the following remarks: ' In the absence of a satisfactory and scientific interpretation, the conflict of opinions between the orthodox and the heretics was decided on another principle than that of exegesis. The apostles, it was said, had received the mysteries of divine truth from our Lord, and had committed them in plain and living words to the apostolic churches. That is a point to which the ancient fathers always recurred. *The written word, they say, is necessarily ambiguous and difficult, but the spoken word of the apostles was clear and transparent.* In the apostolic churches, then, the sum of true doctrine has been handed down in an accurate form; and the consent of the apostolic churches as to the mysteries of faith forms the rule of sound exegesis. Any interpretation of Scripture, say the fathers, is necessarily false if it differs from the *ecclesiastical canon*—that was the technical term which they used— if it differs, that is, from the received doctrinal testimony of the great apostolic churches, such as Corinth, Rome, and Alexandria, in which the word of the apostles was still held to live, handed down by oral tradition' (p. 35).

The sentence which we have put in italics is somewhat modified by that which follows; but its sweeping assertion is not thereby made innocuous. Several of the other sentences give an account of the case which is open to objection as partial, and therefore inaccurate; but they are vague. This one is so definite that it can be tested. We look to the author for his proof. The only proof given by Dr. Smith is in a note at the end of his volume (p. 390), where he says:

'On the *Regula Fidei*, and its connection with the ambiguity of the allegorical interpretation, so keenly felt in controversy with the heretics, compare Diestel, *Geschichte des Alten Testaments in der christlichen Kirche*, p. 38 (Irenæus, Tertullian), p. 85 (Augustine).'

We have already seen that Diestel misrepresents Irenæus; and in so far as Irenæus is concerned, Dr. Smith's statement, which seems to rely on Diestel, lacks foundation. Want of space prevents an examination here of the allegation as regards Tertullian and Augustine. I believe that they—and even Origen— are not fairly liable to the charge conveyed in Dr. Smith's statement. But the question of the supreme position of Scripture in the last quarter of the century is most materially affected by what we learn from Irenæus. And the allegation that Irenæus put any mystical or traditional exegesis whatever above the plain sense of Scripture, I believe to be contrary to fact. The true state of the case I believe to be, that Irenæus put his faith in the written word (the Scriptures), and appealed confidently and incessantly to this as against the heretics. But when they appealed (as the necessities of their position compelled them to appeal) to tradition, he upheld the superiority of the tradition in the Church to anything of the sort which they could claim in their circles. The following positions are easily established in his words :—

1. Our Lord made the apostles the medium of revelation. Book iii. Introduction.

2. The apostles gave the Scriptures as the pillar and ground of the faith. Book iii. 1, § 1.

3. When heretics are convicted from Scripture, they take refuge in tradition, and speak against Scripture as obscure. Book iii. 2, § 1.

4. When we follow their lead and turn to tradition, they disown the tradition found in the Church. Book iii. 2, § 2.

5. But if apostles had known any recondite mysteries, which they taught to a favoured few, those mysteries would have been revealed to the churches· which they founded, and not to the Gnostics. We turn, therefore, to those churches to see. Book iii. 3, § 1.

6. But as a matter of fact, the apostles had no esoteric or secret doctrine: what they learned from the Lord, they taught to all. Book iii. 14, § 2.

7. The heretics, in their claim to have the true tradition, perverted Scripture: what they taught had not the sanction of the Lord, the prophets, and the apostles, in the written word. Book i. 3, § 6; i. 8, § 1; i. 9, § 1, etc.

8. The heritage of the Church is to keep, to guard, and to proclaim the truth committed to her to be preached (i. 10, § 2); and the highest aim of human faculties, and their highest attainment, is to know and expound the great truth of the revelation in the Scripture (i. 10, § 3).

9. In short, the *Rule of Truth is what the Scripture says:* and holding it, we can convict all those who err, manifold though their errors be (i. 22, § 1).

The word tradition (παράδοσις, *traditio*) is used in the fathers as equivalent to 'that which is committed to one's trust,' whether orally or in writing. The same ambiguity, because the same fulness of meaning, is found in St. Paul's use of the word: 'So, then, brethren, stand fast, and hold the *traditions* which ye were taught, whether by word or by epistle of ours' (2 Thess. ii. 15). But to say that Irenæus put an oral tradition as the standard of exegesis over a plain exposition of the written word, is quite another thing, and is inaccurate or misleading.